I0878700

In the Time of the Manaroans

In the Time of the Manaroans

Miro Bilbrough

Victoria University of Wellington Press

VICTORIA UNIVERSITY OF WELLINGTON
TE HERENGA WAKA

Victoria University of Wellington Press
PO Box 600 Wellington
New Zealand
vup.wgtn.ac.nz

First published 2020
Reprinted 2021

ISBN 9781776563128

A catalogue record is available at
the National Library of New Zealand

Printed by Markono Print Media Pte Ltd

for Margaret Beere

Contents

1968

One thing I know, I have an appetite for this man. He is muss-haired, beardy, wears a black oilskin raincoat inside the house and, despite being nameless to me now, is indisputably himself. I can't work him out. He takes his tea cold and clear as a tea-tree-coloured Australian creek. Is it because I have a crush on him that his taste for cold tea is a source of mystery and admiration, or is the cold tea the charismatic thing?

I am four, and there is something alchemical about hot dishes taken cold. A favourite, lonely thing is slicing cold boiled potato with a butter knife on the living-room windowsill, eating slippery-cool starch slice by slice, staring at the openwork of condensation on the windowpane and the weedy green beyond, while my parents' marriage goes to the dogs in the next room.

In the five decades since, I have occasionally turned the coin of Cold Tea & Coat, his musky profile, and wondered if I invented him, a pilgrim or wanderer out of a Grimms' fairy tale illustrated by Arthur Rackham. This early, mythic impression of maleness, scruffy but particular, imprints an archetype of the men I will encounter at my father's house when I next live with him at fourteen, after a separation of seven years.

Built on a floodplain some fifty years previously, my father's Floodhouse is a staging post for a band of hippies who like to break their back-and-forth around the country there. In the Manaroans, named after the remote bay in Pelorus Sound where their commune is based, my engagement with life will abruptly deepen. The sandy shallows of childhood drop, and my feet are, without warning, cycling ocean. I am fourteen and I am drowning *and* waving. Barely at the centre of my own story yet, I am at the periphery of those of some pretty interesting strangers. It doesn't matter that the Manaroans are just passing through; this only increases their savour, inviting me to develop their qualities further in the darkroom of my imagination.

PART 1
My father's house

1978

My father the teetotaller has an open-browed face, decent enough cheekbones, becalmed North Sea eyes that are often elsewhere, and a sudden lightbulb warmth. He wears a homespun skull cap when writing his exercise-book diary in bed—a kapok mattress or three dumped one atop the other to compensate for deformities—in the Floodhouse box room.

Off the kitchen, daylight shuttered by a stand of frowning macrocarpa that run along the west side of the house, the box room is, true to title, full of semi-unpacked cardboard boxes and, supine in stacks and dumps, novels and books of Jung and Sufism bookmarked with the occasional job vacancy for an English teacher, clipped and mailed to my father by his own father, Samuel. This unlikely bedroom–study is lined floor to ceiling with empty, whitewashed tongue-and-groove cupboards that stand over my father as he scribbles in bed. Their towering stance parallels the way his headmaster father once stood over him and psychically still does, prolonging my father's adolescence into his thirties. He's even retained the lined school exercise books of Sam's watch—full, now, of the kind of uncensored interiority that my grandfather would find incomprehensible and obscene.

He likes a house of neglect, my father. He makes little open-air island-nests to feed and read in, to fantasise and hide out in, papery and grubby as those that mice make of shredded paper. More discreet are the actual mice occupying the vacant cupboards that marshall the untidy space.

The Wakamarina

Old farmhouses mingle with one-eyed gold miners' shacks as the valley road ascends between fringes of yellow yarrow, pollen-reeking ragwort and floating micro-domes of Queen Anne's lace. Eventually the thistle- and foxglove-spiked paddocks become numerate with remnant chimneys and the abandoned larders and gold mine shafts—thrillingly treacherous holes that suck you in by the ankles—of long-dead miners and other nineteenth-century chancers.

Gentility passed briefly through but did not stop in the Wakamarina Valley. The late Miss Young, a piano teacher and for a time my father's landlady, was one exception. Up the road and around the bend from the Floodhouse, Miss Young's camellia-fronted villa is now empty. At the end of his marriage, my father stopped here to collect his wits. A few months, and he was gone again. On to the Floodhouse, only a mile down the road but cheaper and deeper in dereliction. Now the gloom-speckled wallpaper, the unattended receiver of Miss Young's party phone, and the lace-frosted windows and fretted wooden eaves that face the valley road are the inheritance of those other lace-makers, spiders. I know this because I have pressed my face to the glass of these old-lady rooms, entered through an unlocked door and, winding the weighty arm of the phone, met the silence of disconnection.

Hidden from but just below the road, the Wakamarina River makes a gladed and pellucid descent in shades of pounamu green, freezing to a fault and sacred to that contemplative high diver with flashing azure wings, the kōtare or kingfisher.

Off road I find other domestic kingdoms every bit as antic and soot-smutted as my father's Floodhouse. Noelene's house is one of these: empurpled by morning glory on the outside; yellowed on the inside with unrefreshed flypapers, which do nothing to cull the flies that tail you obsessively as soon as you enter. Smelling of mouse, stove and lard-coated frying pans, so dim the lack of light is a substance: Noelene's. I'd say this is the smell of dirt poor, but not exclusively, for I encounter it later in the kitchen of the commune landlords, Mick and Edie. The gummy odour of material neglect, then.

My father has come to buy a dozen chook's eggs and brought me sociably along. He offers as barter buttercrunch lettuce from his garden or seconds from his cowshed pottery on the highway. The chooks dance beneath the greasy hem of the kitchen table and flap between Noelene's rooms. There's a warm-skinned man in gumboots inside the unlit kitchen who ambles off to fossick elsewhere, mumbling shyly as he leaves and we enter. Noelene keeps us moving. I glimpse a flame-haired, platform-soled daughter in oblique transit between rooms.

Our stop is brief but performative, the transaction of well-disposed neighbours who share a shyly theatrical bent. They flirt heavy-handedly like a couple of old blokes, my father and Noelene. Or rather it is as if Noelene is the bloke and my father, whose masculinity turns on a dime, some kind of fey hippy ingénue. Noelene's lipstick seems unlikely until you receive her boisterous smile. Her cottage is as rank as her social generosity is contagious. Even her physical ugliness has a brusque radiance. Later my father tells me Noelene is illiterate and I turn this over in uncomprehending grief.

Waiheke Island

My recently separated parents have always romanticised the remote. There was talk of moving to the Outer Hebrides or a Greek island my childhood long. Itching to be anywhere but drearily small-minded New Zealand of the sixties then seventies, their dreaming began in a two-room, red, corrugated-iron beach shack at Pukerua Bay, Wellington, where I spent my infant years. Next came a haunted house on Waiheke Island in the Hauraki Gulf.

In the Waiheke house my mother was often still in bed when I came home from school. There she lay under the shady light of the bamboo blind that she and my father had fashioned from wildly disparate lengths. Running the width of the house, this room was both my parents' bedroom and the living room. Disturbed by the lack of soft furnishings—an expression of arty minimalism that refused to soften the desolate stretch of floorboards—I would bat uncomfortably around, looking for a place to settle.

In that ill-starred house my little brother, Paolo Moses, was born and died a few months later, a cot death. I have a memory of him squalling on yellow velvet under the lemon tree, his little plum-lipped face screwed in distress. The lemon tree whose leaves the underfed goat depilated, tuft by glossy tuft, in the space of one afternoon and a night. I was there for the beginning but gone for the rest of Paolo's short life, gone to my grandmother Margaret's in Wellington. Nothing good ever came about in that house.

Born soon after, my sister was named in the tiny boy's memory but with the feminine version. Paola. She was the good exception that followed his death. Retrospectively, my mother announced that she had decided my sister was going to be the first person she loved, and her utterance entered the family mythology. I was not there to hear it, but I had experienced firsthand the shortfall. By six I openly doubted her love. I had come home from school one day and quizzed her from the foot of the iron bedstead. *You don't love me, do you?*

My mother's refusal to answer burned, guttering like a small house-fire that spread inside me. And spread it did. For much of my adult life this question, and all that it contained, would become a contaminant that I worked around as best I could.

The family story about my move, at seven, away from my parents and new brother, was that my baby teeth had fallen out. Despite homeopathic medication, new teeth refused to grow. I was also having nightmares, waking in terror about the same time every night. Something had to be done.

Later, my father said he was afraid I might die, as if he were making an unwitting transference of the other death, yet to occur, of that tiny peach, Paolo Moses. His fears were an index to the way each of us failed to thrive or prosper under the influence of that house or his and my mother's anempathic marriage.

My own grief at leaving was concentrated in the fate of a paper panda bear I had made at Waiheke Primary School in Ostend. The panda was constructed like a glove puppet: a paper outline coloured in with crayon and then stapled together and stuffed with more paper. A shoebox lined and trimmed with orange and vermillion crêpe paper became a crib for the bear. I adored these creations, but not long after their fashioning I came home one day from school to find I was not going back the next or, indeed, ever again. Why was I bound for the house of my mother's mother? Because she had *offered*, and because she knew, better than I, what kind of trouble I might be in.

In my involuntary departure, the uncollected art project was *the* harrowing source of regret. I wrote a letter from my grandmother's asking after it. My father wrote back that the panda had been given away to another child. I grieved unduly for the talismanic creature cradled in his black-and-white mask and festive bed, the larger grief attaching itself to the small.

After I left Waiheke, my parents' last move was to the Wakamarina Valley. Here their marriage, branching into affairs, ended. My father moved out of their cottage at the top of the valley and down to Miss Young's rental villa. Not long after, my young sister followed him.

One house and a few months on, where this story starts, it is my turn. At fourteen I have fallen out with my grandmother and down a rabbit hole into my father's unknown.

A brief history

How did I get here, exactly? I rang my father from the red phone box on the footpath outside my grandmother's, praying that she wouldn't spring me inside my emergency-coloured beacon. She doesn't, because down inside the house below street level Grandmother Margaret is also ringing my father, but from the landline.

Three days later my father arrives to ferry me back to live in Canvastown, Marlborough. I know I am about to fall off the grid. The grid, as I know it, comprises a circle of girlfriends from relatively stable middle-class homes, my A-student niche, my weekend prowls, life as my grandmother's last daughter. Despite my scarlet phone call, I feel I have no real say in the abrupt termination of these things.

Recently, though, I have had a bit to say—too much even. Sent to my room or to bed intolerably early for answering back, *You pig!* is my go-to grenade hurled down the varnished wood-veneer hall, past the black Bakelite phone fixed to the wall. *You pig!* bounces off the closed lounge door with swastika provocation carved into the white paint by a mutinous Uncle Martin, three years my senior. Under instruction, Martin has just slammed the door. They're behind it now, uncle and grandmother, legs stretched luxuriously from hire-purchase sofa, television turned up loud to tune me out.

I am a storm in a teacup. The teacup is 46A Upland Rd, Kelburn, and a childhood life cosily contained inside my pensioner grandmother's flat and immunised from the world that, increasingly, calls its siren call. Sloshing around inside is me: a fantastically restless and thanklessly horny brew passing in an unflattering teenage body. Adolescence has hit my mood centres and transformed me into an unruly devastation of discontents, pining for what, *I don't know*. Sometimes I focus the yearning on a boy but there are precious few within reach. I go to Wellington Girls' College, after all. More often the yearning remains unfocused, roving around inside my body.

My legs know things. Other things. They trek me around convolvulus backstreets where I stare into student flats and imagine other lives over long weekend hours. Only my drama teacher, Diane McCarthy, engages me as an equal: at school, in drama club, and by phone. Thinking, despite her evident marriage, that Diane might be a lesbian, Grandmother Margaret presses the switch hook and disconnects the lingeringly chatty, extra-mural calls I receive from her. My grandmother has it wrong about my drama teacher. Her transgressions are not sexual but hierarchical. Instead of treating me as her pupil, Diane McCarthy honours me as her confidante.

*

As for my father, thanks to geographical distance and affinity, he has been a letter-writing icon loved from afar. In seven years, I've only seen him and my mother a handful of times. Before I leave my grandmother's, she warns me never to undress in the same room as him. That sets me thinking. My grandmother is a communist, far from libertarian. Her view of my parents is a lurid mash-up of warnings that I disregard as best I can. Against my better judgement, her cautioning insinuates itself into my modest baggage.

The actual luggage consists of an encyclopaedic *Birds of The World*; a gold-lacquer musical jewellery box—minus twirling ballerina—that Margaret's youngest daughter, Aunt Melissa, has passed on to me; a pink sateen eiderdown; and a solitary blue towel. The towel is judiciously extracted from 46A's Tardis-like linen cupboard, inside which I once built womb-like forts, and on whose roof Martin liked to sit in meditation pose, a phony sannyasi with two wings of glossy chocolate hair.

Three decades later the exhausted remnant of that well-travelled blue towel—a fray-fringed square—will still exist in my father's self-effacing linen stack.

Tiger stripes

When I was a small, serious child, Margaret called me *The Christian*, which may have been a shade dry coming from a communist but not entirely. It was I who routinely patched up the quarrels in our household of three, the first to seek forgiveness or to forgive. Passionate in mollification, my small chubby hand advancing into the fraught air—*Shake!*—could be counted on to bring my antagonist around.

I had good reason to be a peace-broker. I knew that simmering family conflict could have extreme outcomes, for that was how I came to live at Grandmother Margaret's aged seven. I could barely endure a squabble, much less the incendiary device of my grandmother's rage, by dint of which saucepans or teacups of water and lethally unsleeved vinyl spun across the room or out the kitchen window as Martin or I ran. Now, in her summary operatic style, Margaret has as good as flung *me* out the window. Poor impulse control notwithstanding, she has her reasons.

Expulsion carries echoes of that earlier leave-taking, of leaving my parents' house for Grandmother Margaret's for a holiday that lasted seven years. One minute I was at Rocky Bay, scoffing sandy fly cemeteries—sticky slabs of raisin-studded biscuit—straight out of the packet with my visiting grandmother and Uncle Martin. Next, I was on a plane to join them in their two-bedroom Wellington flat where Aunt Melissa, ballet dancer and scholar of Ancient Greek, also lived.

Once there, I shared the one bedroom containing three single beds and generations: grandmother, daughter and granddaughter. Martin slept down the hall in the dungeon, a narrow room of tacit gloom. Between calico curtains hand-painted with *Long Live the People's Republic!* in Chinese characters, a prospect of damp concrete steps and too-close fence undercut the rhetoric. Perhaps this is where Martin first fell to depression.

I was nervous about how Melissa, who supplemented my grandmother's pension with a librarian's earnings, would stand my arrival and the subsequent overcrowding, but I don't hear a word of complaint. I am nervous about everything, but the close quarters of 46A are a comfort after the endless, spooky savannahs of my parents' Waiheke house. In my new, shared

bedroom, distance is so negligible that, if I have a nightmare, I can launch myself straight into Margaret's bed with just one touchdown on the carpet in between.

Reaching my grandmother's bed, I like to dive under the sheets to feel the bevelled callus worn to a knife-edge on the bottom of her little toe. Margaret claims to leave it this way for the cutting of bread. I adore this joke, and hope that I, too, might grow such a thing. My grandmother is nothing if not generous with the ruin of her body. Tiger's stripes, she calls the lines on her forehead, inviting me to covet the spoils of ageing. And I do. I am within the grand-matriarchal circle of kindness now.

When I gain in confidence and familiarity, I will sometimes kiss Aunt Melissa's manicured hand. I am a bookworm interested in the male roles—in gallantry, too. They have so much more to do, boys and sons, wizards, wayfarers and princes, and I have been blithely identifying with their universal 'I' since I stepped out into the transcendent world of fiction at four. Like most of my sex I have been a gender-deft reader since earliest girlhood.

Admiration for the cross beauty that is my young aunt notwithstanding, I am acutely aware, even at seven, that it is she who finances my new life. In my grandmother's shoestring household, you come to economic consciousness quick. As for the hand kissing, Melissa is bemused. She thinks me a courtier with a courtier's excessive form and on-the-make motive. In fact, I *am* on the chase with all its rush and risk, ardour and hunger. A pattern for life.

My grandmother's house at 46 Upland Road is a three-storey green wooden layer-cake stepped into a plunging bank that overlooks a residential valley called *The Glen*. With its curlicued ceiling and prismatic view from front bay windows, our flat is the lovely jam in the middle. The flat downstairs, the damp-leaked bottom sponge, is rented by another of my grandmother's daughters, Amanda, and her husband, David. Of their three children—Rebecca, Ben and Sean—it is ostensibly Becky—piquant featured, prone to spending the morning in bed, addicted to puns—I go to see. Whizzing down the concrete steps, I experience a nervous thrill at the fug of sophistication generated by caustically youthful Aunt Amanda, founder of grassroots organisation Wellington Tenants' Protection, never without a gold carton of Benson & Hedges in hand. As I see it *46B* is Modern Life at one enviable remove. Traffic between the flats is constant.

Back upstairs at 46A, life amidst the oatmeal carpets and anodyne wallpaper is a culture shock after the troubling animism of my mother's fierce anti-furnishings and her habit of travelling naked through the day. Uncomfortable with comfort, unaccustomed, I will have to learn it. Quick smart I do.

When, occasionally, one of my mother's letters arrives, the first journey my hand takes is from the letterbox to my nose. On the paper I can smell the ants that race up and down the Rocky Bay trees and the raw timber walls of my last home, and the oil with which my mother lacquers her body. Redolent of these things and so much more the envelope produces a physical wave of longing far greater than any word within. Gigantic words they are too.

I am learning tidy cursive at school, linking letters to order, marshalling them along the line. Cursive is a religion, my primary school teachers its clerics. To my prim infant eye, my mother has an embarrassingly outsize hand.

My mother's daughter

When I arrived at my grandmother's she was exactly the age I am as I write these words. Fifty-four. I do not know if she was through menopause, nor, at the time, did I have an inkling of such a thing. The word was never spoken at 46A in my hearing. If it had been, I would have parsed its strangely literal three-parter and committed it to memory. I kept an ear out for multisyllables. Always.

It was, however, impossible to miss that Margaret had withdrawn what little confidence she had in men as husbands and lovers. *That rum bunch!* No man came *courting*, as she called it. Her lambent gaze and radical politics seemed to diminish the few stray male contemporaries I ever caught in the same room as her. It was left to her children to find her romantic. And we did. How difficult it must have been for Martin to grow into a member of that disappointing species, *man*, so empathically aligned was he with his mother.

When my grandmother and I began falling out, Martin was straining so badly at the business of living that my grandmother hadn't the emotional reserves to do with me as well. Since I arrived, she had marked the signs of small-girl sexuality, those involuntary signifiers of my mother before me. She would frown on the small hand—mine—that sometimes sought out my vagina through my clothes. She equated this to my parents' lack of decorum and *unhealthy fixation on the sexual parts*. This antagonised my loyalties and made my vagina assume exactly the energetic focus she was hoping to stifle.

When I was twelve or so, I came home on the Plimmerton train, from a girlfriend's house, in tan nylons and an orange wool mini with gold chains on the pockets. Gifts of Trish. The sensation of encasing nylons, the train ride alone in re-imagined skin—how contemporary! When I reached home, briny with the Plimmerton esplanade, ice cream and the vacant looks of boys on bikes, my grandmother thought I looked *cheap*. Precisely.

It was from Trish—a short, chubby sensualist with fudge-brown eyes behind a fringe, and indulgent working-class parents—that I adopted the mid-seventies braid belt, knotted in front with ties hanging down. There was no way of getting this past Margaret's censorial eye. She scolded that the belt must be knotted at the side, not the front where it pointed genital-ward.

My grandmother had her mind on predators. Wellington was rich in flashers at windows and wankers along Oriental Parade. But there were also generational repetitions in her fear. My grandmother monstered my mother's flagrant sexual charisma at sixteen (not that *I* had inherited it), giving her marching orders early. This was rich, given Margaret's own magnetic beauty and historically expressive sexuality. Recording this, I wonder afresh about her unhappy relationship with the middle daughter who was to become my mother.

When my grandmother was an old lady, and I had taken up the status of occasional, polite visitor to her house, she would confide that her own mother picked her up at five or six and said, *I will never love you*. It may have been an overburdened mother's fit of pique but from this express antipathy my grandmother never fully recovered. That rejection became a central object, one that would ripple, daughter to daughter, down the years.

My grandmother's mother, Great-grandmother Lily, spent much of her later years in a mental asylum. In a family photograph taken when she was young, before the ill-starred events of marriage or maternity, Lily Beere née Winter appears an exquisitely solemn, almost spectral Edwardian beauty in

a white sashed shift, plaited brunette hair coiled around her head. *Here I am*, her candid stare seems to declare as she rests her arm on that of her neighbouring father's chair—*and not*.

I knew little of Lily but for the intricate pencil drawings of winged and vaulted geometries she made during her long incarceration. The drawings, glossy with webs of graphite, lasted my whole childhood in a dog-eared Manila folder I consulted without ever quite knowing what I was looking at. Perplexingly intimate labours. The interiors of Gothic cathedrals. Anxious, celestial shapes. Pencil mantras. Bonsai rages. The inside of my great-grandmother Lily's head.

Much later, in the grip of her mother's remembered vow or a desire to exculpate the horror of Lily's fate, or both, my grandmother burned the folder full of pencil stalagmites. This enraged my mother, who felt, quite rightly, the abstract genius of this testimony was not Margaret's to burn. More, that Lily's artistry and even temperament had passed to her.

But to go back—or forward, actually. Margaret's censure of my adolescent mother's sexuality failed as it was bound to. After an abortion, my mother became, almost immediately, pregnant again, this time with me. The way she tells it, my father was, despite the fact that he came under the Sign of the Weedy Intellectual in his unprepossessing duffel coat, someone who might look after her. And so, wildly unsuitable as they felt each other to be, barely twenty years old apiece, my parents married. A disastrous move except that it produced me, and then, seven years on, my sister.

In the middle flat at 46 Upland Rd, where life has been so jammy for her grandchild, Margaret is afraid I will become my extravagantly uncurtailable mother: original, antipathic, creative, obsessed with vaginas and penises, with female

Christs with genital stigmata, with orifices, wounds and transcendently fleshy portals in her art. So many vaginas and erect penises that they have exited the subliminal discourse, and the picture plane, into plain sight.

As for me, I am my mother's daughter and, at fourteen, I am in the process of shedding my chubby childhood cloak for more volatile skin.

Uncle Martin

It is not as if Margaret doesn't have enough on her hands as a solo mother in her early sixties to Martin. Sensitive, radical, dyslexic, fervently anti-school, pianist manqué, *Guinness Book of Records* nerd, entombed-in-asphyxiating-silences Martin is also a vegetarian who converts my grandmother to the cause—to many causes, in fact, including his own. The last, late-born of my grandmother's to a brief swansong of a Hungarian husband, Martin is held extra close in her esteem. Technically my uncle, for seven years Martin is a vivid, slightly remote brother to me.

I worship him shyly. I am attracted to him. I am embarrassed that I do so well in school and he doesn't. I think him brilliantly funny. *And she was walking down the road when a ten-tonne truck swerved and ran over her*, Martin broadcasts at breakneck speed and volume whenever I tell tales to Margaret. He has just demonstrated a Chinese burn on me, and yet I subside into laughter at this other, fictionally fatal maiming. I don't mind him practising stand-up on me.

As I get older, however, it is impossible to miss the fact that, between flare-ups of Pythonesque humour, Martin boils down into the pose of a kind of handsome puppet. Pale,

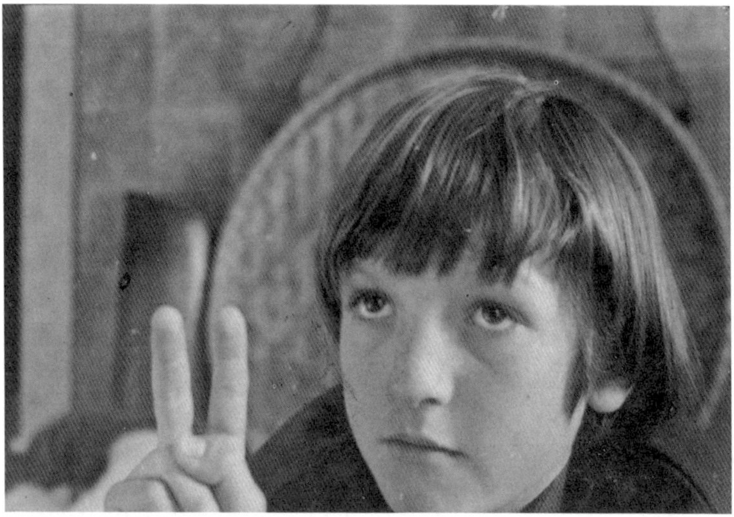

with bright dark eyes and a straight, sensuous nose with an attractive bump that owes much to his Magyar ancestors, the older Martin gets the more he is prone to go slack, as if someone has dropped the wooden cross holding him up and let the animating strings slacken. Then, he is given to a prolonged armchair stillness that is deeply uneasy to be around.

In this stultification my facility with words is an aggravation. Margaret accuses me of being pretentious, of deliberately going after the biggest words around. It is true—I do. The injustice is that she misconstrues my native joy in language as an insult to her son's silence. Years later, my mother will write a poem in which she credits my word facility with the fact that she got stuck in a lavatory with *Roget's Thesaurus* when she was pregnant. This family tale pleases us both. *Lavatory* is a word gleaned from my grandmother. Class affectation or just a word with more aural charisma than toilet? Both, I think.

These days Martin would be diagnosed with depression and anxiety and, even more likely, as bipolar, but it is the mid-seventies and Martin attributes his suffering to class oppression. It is true that we are working class, and that Martin lacks the kind of networked opportunities that the middle-class children of our privileged university suburb enjoy. It is also true that the emotional disappointment of his estranged father produces a pain acute, then chronic, as toothache. There is fury, too. At school his *Workers of the World Unite* rhetoric gets him into fights. As an early leaver, with a job in the boiler rooms of Parliament, it gets him fired. With acutely high arches, piano-player fingers and an ever-present sense of class outrage, Martin is not a natural fit for manual work or for sucking up or for climbing down from an argument. This idealistic inflexibility is cause for great admiration in our household.

Then there is hair. Both he and Cousin Sean sport theirs long and proud. Sean's is a curling mass of wayward vectors, Martin's shoulder length and lank as any rock star's. It is the early seventies; hair is unusually significant and, besides, both teenagers know that politics are performative. They delight in routinely being mistaken for girls by adoring old ladies and, less adoringly, train conductors.

But in Martin's case all paths lead back to the turquoise sofa at 46A. There is palpable suffering in his sentence, and in his chocolate-eyed person, and the women of our household gather around. Melissa brings him home-cooked Chinese meals on a tray, courtesy of Lun, the Malaysian student–husband with whom she has moved in downstairs. She insists that Martin's depression and immobilisation are a side effect of being a vegetarian who fails to approach diet with sufficient rigour. Ahead of her time in these matters, Melissa has diagnosed his sweet tooth as one problem, lack of protein as another.

I respect Martin's armchair sorrow, resent the right of primogeniture in culinary play, and covet the exotic single-serve portions that float up from downstairs. A refugee from my parents' wholefoods, I have been cooking from a stack of colour-plate gourmet cards I found chucked in the back of the cutlery drawer not long after I arrived. I thrill to the exotic, have exquisite tastebuds, can identify the narcotic waft of cardamom from twenty paces.

My grandmother settles the issue of my exclusion from downstairs meals with a disparaging flick of her famously empathic regard. *You can live on your hump like a camel*, she says. The verdict is in. I am chubby, my pot belly is my hump, and I have no need for Red Cross Asian. I suck Margaret's fat-hating up.

Busy Beaver, grandmother calls me another day, and now

she sounds admiring or only gently satiric. I have prominent front teeth and I *am* busy. My shins are covered in bruises from falling on the concrete steps as I enter or leave our flat. When not serenely dreaming, I rush. I like art projects, séances, acting, reading, going places and talking. I am deceptively shy, dedicated to equity, bossy. If there are four sweets and three friends, I spin the fourth Jelly Baby into the gutter.

Under my red Lurex poncho, I *do* have a pot. I may be ashamed of the humps and bumps, the manifestation of appetite in my body, but I am not giving appetite up.

Harold Wilson

Wiry-limbed and witted, authority averse, Sean appears drawn in a hurry. In this Sean reminds me of my first love, the serially defiant Ginger of Edward Ardizzone's children's book *Tim and Ginger*. Was it the drawing I was mad for or the boy? At five or six, I couldn't have quite said. Clearly that scurrying pen line *was* the boy. I am compelled by characters on the run, as if launched in a race against their own wits and other, crueller forces, too.

A dynamic irritant in the eye of any jurisdiction—family, school, New Zealand Railways—my cousin Sean is real enough. Joyriding on the train home from Onslow College, his scruffy, insouciant aspect routinely piques the attention of the guards.

Name?

Harold.

Surname?

Wilson, Sean returns, noting the thickness of his interlocutor in failing to recognise that he has given him the name of the current British prime minister.

The main point of this incident, as far as Sean is concerned, is that he is briefly the talk of the family, his hardest-to-please audience. Amanda takes on a raptor aspect and her eyes disappear in ambiguous smiles as she scolds her son for spending his ticket money on *What exactly? Pot? Fags?* Each is, for once, glancingly satisfied with the other. Where else does Sean get those reflexes from but his mother.

For Martin, the impressive thing is his nephew's front. When I ask, newly arrived at 46A and testing the local moral ground, why Martin doesn't spend some of the change from a pint of milk or pound of butter on lollies, Martin replies, *Because I lick my lips when I lie.* I am seven. Martin, ten. Home-schooled in deceit around diet and compensatory treats, I am the better liar. Even more adept is Sean.

My cousin has eyelashes as long as a giraffe's and eyes whose size and sensitivity are enhanced by glasses. I note the eyelashes in particular because, like all children raised on Disney cartoons, I am obsessed with the relation of eyelash length to beauty. All three cousins possess optimal length. The fact that the elbows are out of Sean's unravelling sweaters, like my remembered father's, further captures my attention.

Sean returns the favour by declaring that were he to marry anyone in the family it would be me. We are of that age when such things are weighed up and considered, when spawning haemophiliacs is an interesting option. But it is Martin who is Sean's peer and ally in any scrape or rebellion. Sean is at least as angry as Martin but more agile, which stands him in good stead for a future life as a lawyer and, even later, a change of gender. It helps that he has the gift of the gab.

Once, I am invited along by uncle and cousin to poke in the front teeth of Becky's baby doll, using a stick sourced from the blackberry gully that abuts 46A. The doll is hollow so that, stoved-in, the teeth rattle around inside, taking the place of her expensive bleat. Sean has seen to the voice box, too. There was something aggravating about the hard, beige, plastic blubber of the unsexed doll and her complacent blue stare. Our pleasure in this malicious destruction outlives the shame, although I know it is wrong that Sean and Martin are automatically fingered for it and I am not. I am belatedly sorry for Becky, too. What is wrong with me? It does not occur to me that I might be exacting revenge on the doll for my mother's refusal, on non-negotiable aesthetic grounds, to let me own one.

Not long after, Sean climbs up the drainpipe from the concrete yard at the back of Amanda and David's flat to my shared bedroom window. There his face appears, eyes brightening at the sight of me and a girlfriend in séance at an occasional table. We have ringed the varnished top with the alphabet, and I am slyly nudging the glass with my fingertip. Shamed by Sean's self-insertion, I grab a coat hanger and strike his fingers taloned over the sill. He protests, eyes harum-scarum, and falls a metre or three into a cactus planted in a chamber pot directly below. Sean dines out on the cacti needles and shards of china in his bum for a long time after. I am confronted by my impulses once more. What kind of girl am I?

The Terrace

Aunt Amanda has moved her family to the draughty top floor of a Victorian villa, isolated on its own rise on the Terrace by slimy wooden steps with the occasional slat missing. This Gothic inner-city pile has been purchased at a reduced price thanks to a recent murder. Bloodstains and chalk markings map the lounge-room floor, and there is a wall-size mirror in whose visage the crime undoubtedly took place and, in my mind, takes place still. I am glad that past reflections cannot speak or transmit their visual signals. And yet, in a way they do.

Once the upstairs is made more habitable, I sometimes stay over for the weekend. Sunday morning, Uncle David, a deliberate man of glass-bead eyes and defining cleft chin, will bring us kids strong tea and wine biscuits in the bunk beds. It is here that I discover dunking, losing disc-shaped continents to silt. Sometimes my cousin Becky and I follow silly voices down the hall to join Amanda listening to the Goons in bed. Despite such pleasures, I never really know where I am in this bohemian-chic, burlap-walled household. The barest and most ad hoc of renovations proceeds and digresses, digresses and proceeds over the years, much like the marriage of Amanda and David. You have to mind the odd sticking-up nail, ancestor of the vanished carpet, in the unsheathed floorboards.

In the evenings the smoke-wreathed talk at the dining table is sardonic, left wing and enabled by cask red wine. Inserting puns into discussion of reactionaries and slum landlords, Becky is blithely accommodated to her parents' discourse, as self-contained and elegantly low output as a cat. In private, she and I read to each other from a book of abrupt short poems by Spike Milligan, a volume that remains in circulation between us for years. There's even a demented LP of his; though, in this case, I discover it is possible to surfeit on Spike.

Eventually Amanda will move out of the upstairs and in downstairs with George, the lawyer with whom she and David share both the original house purchase and, in the founding of Wellington Tenants' Protection, a history of activism. After

this, things will go on much as before, minus George's live-in former girlfriend, co-founder Pauline, and with the addition of a Wagner soundtrack, red brocade curtains and a white-and-pink English bull terrier called Frieda—none of which are quite as ironic as Amanda affects.

Last love of the lastborn

At 46A Martin has developed ingrown toenails, excruciating accumulations and deformations that have to be operated on repeatedly. Our lives together have begun to feel insufferably claustrophobic. When his frustration isn't practised on the wood-veneer panels of Grandmother Margaret's hallway there is the palpable sense that at any minute it might turn harmfully inward.

Although I do not explicitly factor Martin's troubles into the abrupt move-along my grandmother gives me when I am fourteen and he is seventeen, I am half aware of their unacknowledged ground. If I fall prey to thinking I am the centre of the narrative, the alignment of Martin and his mother gives this the lie as the war inside his head draws them ever closer.

In the year he turns twenty-one, Martin falls hard for a blond work colleague who seeks him out as confidant then lover and intimate third-party witness to her failing marriage. The *blond* descriptor carries heightened charge in my grandmother's household where all are brunettes, and I find out little else about Martin's lover. I am back in Wellington, a design student, and Martin is intensely, visibly, in that otherworldly place people in love go.

He is full of certainty and frail incandescence whenever I visit 46A from my flat across town to watch the latest music videos on *Radio with Pictures*. The television has been placed so that my grandmother can watch from bed. There is a grey velvet club armchair for visitors, and the same view of the blackberry-engulfed gully, the classically shady and unforgiving Wellington prospect I once inspected most mornings on waking. It is in this visitor's chair I sit, across the room from the uncle–brother whom I semi-idolised and fell in and out with as a child.

When the woman he is having an affair with goes back to her husband, Martin hangs himself outside that same bedroom window behind which I once slept alongside his mother and sister, and where Margaret will now sleep alone.

I am at my Bidwill Street flat when I receive the call from Uncle David. He has a fit-for-broadcasting voice, deep and faintly grainy, with a strategic sense of when to be silent. I hang on to these reassuring qualities as best I can, but the voice has terrible things to say.

Outside my lounge window the cracked concrete of the pocket yard is sickeningly unreliable. Inside, the Beatles LPs that once belonged to Martin are propped along the skirting boards. How can these things be here and Martin not? Every *thing* is a container for the violence of what he has done.

I don't remember much of the funeral. Someone picks me up to drive to Martin's cremation. At the wake I clear plates, replenish sandwiches and wash dishes in the tiny kitchen of 46A, round upon round of dishes, as if I am washing all the dishes that Martin and I dodged and whinged about my childhood long and that Margaret sometimes even paid us to do. I keep myself busy amidst the clutter of female bodies that come and go: my ever-capable aunts', the listing ship of my grandmother's. This loss is so much bigger than any of us, all I can do is serve it.

At the centre is the interrupted love story between Martin and his mother, Margaret. My grandmother is as close to a force of nature as I have ever encountered, and so is the tide of her grief. Periodically that year, and for some to come, I will wake sharply in my bed across town with an awareness of what it feels like to be her. Calling first thing to see how she is, I will find it has been one of *those* nights, the unthinkable ones when she is swallowed whole. Then, selfishly, I will be reassured that we are closer than either of us imagines.

Stink materials

My sister is seven when she is posited at Miss Young's rented villa. From there it is a skip and a hop to my father's next camp, the Floodhouse. My sister arrives directly from our mother's, the house where my father and she once cohabited in unhappy approximation of a family. Since then my mother's lover, Heinz, an arcane and crafty man of heavy sensuality, a beekeeper who wears his hair in two deft plaits, has moved a mile or so up the valley to take my father's place.

I arrive just a few months after my sister, an interloper seven years her elder. Some days her prominent brow, still decked in the memory of my mother's elaborately plaited coiffures, is thunderous with separation. The emotional lives of adults are amateur and messy. My sister is as unsure of what she's doing in my father's tip as I am.

I like her resolute looks, and her oil pastels of princesses as imperious as their author in oversized vermillion lips, emerald shifts and wings. Once or twice she presents me with these crayon familiars. In turn, she will become the subject of Marlborough Girls' College photography assignments in black and white. But only our representations mingle. Concentrating on survival our flesh and blood selves remain discrete. There is a sense of category error about our sudden arrival that each of us is powerless to correct. Instead of bringing us closer, however, the sensation keeps us isolated. We admire and disdain each other from a distance, secretly vying for pre-eminence in my father's affections: I with precocious conversation and my body's sudden outages; she with the wonderland of her drawings and her rages.

One afternoon after school my sister kicks over the piss-filled potty she has let suppurate for a week in her bedroom: the humble protest materials at her disposal. Stink materials. This is a fact I am forbidden ever to mention, and therefore do.

I find out she takes lunch with the spiders and rubble, a book for company, in the foundations of the tiny country primary school she attends at road's end. *Hippy kid!* the other children accuse. And so, she finds herself taking solitude and honey cake underneath the classroom during breaks. I am chagrined that the valley kids could disrespect or bully this small, sovereign character but, then, she is so soberly other to their experience: two micro rat's-tail plaits mounted above her forehead like a crown, literature her refuge.

For my part I have a body that refuses to cooperate. I don't shit for a week after I arrive on the ferry, fresh from expulsion from 46A. My father's shock diet of soya beans and lentils and salad sprinkled with kelp and dandelion greens clinches it. Not to mention the architectural and sanitary dereliction of the Floodhouse. I am held in, impacted, packed so tight I don't know if I'll ever be able to let a shit or anything else out again.

The lavatory is out back, a collection of rickety boards impersonating a shack erected over a hole in the ground, bum-wipe newspaper handy. Hippy visitors call our long drop *the shitter.* Precisely. I can't believe where I've landed, but I say nothing about this. Hunch around the house in my concealing cardigan instead.

Wiener schnitzel

Once a week my father heats a volume of river water in a copper outside and carries buckets and supplementary saucepan- and kettle-full to the afterthought that passes as a bathroom. With no running water at the Floodhouse for drinking or bathing, the river provides. Bearing ever-diminishing vessels, like some kind of riff on the three bears, my sister and I participate in the hot water convoy. My sister's ginger slip of cat, Joey, named after the Dylan song, wends in the slipstream. The bathroom is so permeable, so outside in, that my father has to lay an old plank from door to bath's edge in order to cross the primeval soup that passes for floor. Bath hour is a heroic effort made on his daughters' account. Crouched in the warm rusty puddle between yellowing bath walls, candlelight hurling labile shadows at the outlying everglades of the room, I fail to appreciate his labour. It's a spooky experience, its cleansing properties unconvincing.

My father tries to ease the horror of transition. Once a week, he agrees, I can eat the thin-cut wiener schnitzel that was a staple of my grandmother's. I sense the concession this Jesus-sandalled vegetarian must make to enter the Havelock butcher. He is adaptable my father, not one to stand on ideology or, in this case, cost, even though he's barely making do on a solo parent's benefit.

I am adamant about meat. A zealot when it comes to equity, my sister frowns over the special dietary dispensation but is unwilling to participate in the consumption of baby cow.

On my father's side

Short on the fruits of the industrial age, there is a surplus of time to think at the Floodhouse. No heat at the turn of a dial or water at the turn of a tap. No maraschino cherries to chase with fingers around the fruit salad tin, or Hanna-Barbera cartoons to consume while lying on carpeted living-room floor. This state of abruptly confiscated resources leaves me percolating inside giant spots of time. I am not the only one. For hours at a stretch each of us kills time in the separate rooms of the house and our heads.

Unmoored by recent separation from my mother, my father writes in his diary and does paintings of the naked-and-no-longer-young sporting too-long arms and wrong-coloured faces (blue, orange). I find the paintings as queasy as intended but not as droll. I am quick to revulsion. My father once attended Elam art school where Colin McCahon was his teacher, although he claims he was unable to learn anything from a man who had so little connection with or sympathy for other people. You never get anywhere in my family for dropping a name unless you give it a bit of a drubbing.

He likes to say he only married my mother to get his books back. She'd borrowed them and he didn't know how to ask for them again. Never mind that she was pregnant with me. He recalls the lump of coal she wore wired to her finger, and that when she walked down Majoribanks Street she was the object of wolf whistles from the building site he laboured on over the university holidays. It is hard to imagine my father, who suffers from acute vertigo, on a building site. Easier to visualise the lump of coal complementing the sloping kohl lines that framed my mother's twenty-year-old eyes.

My father also recalls a dress she cut from a cardboard box. It was 1962 and she was among the first intake of design school students at Wellington Polytechnic. Marrying my mother, her own avant-garde creation, must have been a real *fuck you* to his conventional Howick parents. There was never any talk of love, on either side.

For the record, my father's mother was a painter too. Of scenic bridges with poplars and other muted views. A Sunday painter. Once or twice I stood on a chair and peered into the small, skilful watercolours hung behind glass high on the Howick grandparents' walls. With a child's unforgivingly direct sense of colour and form, I judged the paintings not much less insipid than the wallpaper. And yet something about the placement of Grandmother Susan's paintings, and the attention with which they were rendered, marked them out as an activity blessedly beyond the purview of her husband. It was hard to resist the feeling that had gentle, sensitive Grandmother Susan made a happier marriage she might not have been as timid or self-diluting as she was in company with quick-to-ignite Sam. The elemental mix of the two was unconducive to self-realisation. Even as an eight-year-old, negotiating the many rules and stipulations of their suburban home, I knew that.

And yet. The photographs my father keeps of his mother offer a counterweight to this micro-story of marital oppression and to my childish perceptions. Optimism keeps ready company with vulnerability in this visual record. Almost never without a hat and gloves, Susan appears chipper, trim, infectiously available. Having escaped the house, she seizes the hour.

I admire the woman I see here. She is irresistible.

Mythologies spring up in families about traits and talents: about who got what and from where. Raised for half my childhood in the house of my mother's mother the tap root of self felt extravagantly matrilineal. In those years my identification with the paternal side stopped at my romanticised, much-missed-and-missing father. Visiting the regimented, *other*-grandparental rooms; eating a sugared grapefruit from the tree that crouched on Grandfather Sam's lawn; keeping pace with the trolley—*so dowdy*—Grandmother Susan wheeled to the suburban shops, I did not feel related so much as dislocated and bored.

I can see that Granny Margaret's urban values—a pot-pourri of communism, own-brand feminism and modernist aesthetics—unfairly coloured my vision. Looking, for the first time, at certain photographs of Susan Bilbrough née McKenzie, something passes through her gaze into mine and I recognise the feeling of readiness, of zestful know-how that, on a good day, I take to meet my students.

Susan died of cancer in her sixties. Her blue eyes, clots of bright hyacinth in a powdered face, came down the line to her sons—my father and his older brother Alan—and to my sister. I have my mother's hazel ones.

After Susan's death Grandfather Sam kept up his disciplinary schedules of mowing, pruning and plucking; of Daffodil Association and Annual Show; of bossing and administrating other local societies beyond our ken or care. He was as tall, knobble-limbed and hierarchical as ever, but we hadn't realised how equably sociable instincts roosted alongside his temper. That no-holds-barred smile should have alerted us, that sudden swoop he would take to beam into my face from his superior elevation. Even more surprising to my father was that, widowed, the old man was pursued by several neighbourhood women.

Sam resisted the live-in arrangement evermore but enjoyed a mutual understanding with a vigorous woman of bottlebrush hair and ready humour. *The Goat*, my mother called Grandfather Sam when I was small. In spite of his air of disapproval, she felt he had lustful eyes.

My father is murderously cheerful about the end of his marriage. It is as if he has just escaped an especially strict school—not Sam's this time. At thirty-eight the gift of so much unsupervised time is at once giddy and a dead weight. The involuntary custody of first my sister and then me soon sees to that.

When he bumps into my mother and Heinz at the General Store, or when dropping off my sister for visits, there is a desultory little to say. A rancorous politesse holds on all sides. If we are present, my sister will instinctively align with my mother. I hang at the edges, witness and unhappy little human knot.

When he is done wrangling dinner on the mother lode of the wood range or washing up with an enamel pan in the plug-less porcelain sink, I find my father tired, private of habit,

14

unusual of conversation, obviously benign. Nobody has to cajole me to wipe the dishes because they are never wiped but remain scaffolded on the soggy wooden benchtop till needed.

My grandmother's fearful insinuations about incest, her parting gift, languish and die a natural death too.

I begin to focus on my surroundings, to see what they will render. Allowed the use of a camera for the weekend by the art department at Marlborough Girls' College, I stalk my sister, securing her agreement to pose on the overgrown lawn under Miss Young's camellia. Once there, my sister resembles an ancestral tintype of probity and seriousness. We *are* living in the past, a mini branch of ancestors sawn off from the family tree. I pin the study-in-grey-tones on my bedroom wall.

The smell of things

When we emerge from our under-furnished rooms, we might notice that the surrounding land gives off waves of mucky scent. A field run to pennywort, crushed underfoot, rises up, narcotically minty. The spermy smell of so many young, green things prevails. River-cold, frost-astringent, rain-bitten, mud-whiffy, fennel-seeding, silage and birds' nests: the smell of the Wakamarina Valley. The green is so green it is a drug, an emerald intoxicant that fills eye and nostril. In the middle of my father's Great and Unusual Mess, the mess I have landed in, there is this *this*ness.

The fog off the river is thick as phlegm when I walk to catch one of three consecutive school buses. Fog drapes a clammy cloak that swallows everything, including my Treks—the trendy lace-up beige suede shoes with an inside-out seam running from toe to tongue that I departed Granny

Margaret's in. Then there is a cow. Parting mist curtain with noir nose. Then four cows with shade-fringed, black-lamp eyes, crowding the fence to see who I am. It's so nice the way they bolt *Hello* towards me. Thank God for the fence.

Punctum

Not long after I arrive, I overhear my father telling the district nurse, who has come to administer an enema to my constipation, how articulate his elder daughter is, as if, thereby, countering the one withholding with the other fluency.

In my grandmother's flat I used too many big words. In my father's house there is space for my voice to range. I have found an audience in this thirty-seven-year-old sitting up in bed in a beanie, eating omelette with a Fujiyama of kelp on the side.

Besides my recently restored father, however, I don't have a friend yet. Each morning of the week I climb off the minibus that drives local students east from Canvastown to Havelock, the fishing village on State Highway 6, to connect with another bus that carries us to Blenheim and to Marlborough Boys' or Girls'. In my case, to complete the last half of the fifth form. In Havelock's tiny main street, a waiting scrum of would-be alphas tackles the bus door. Girls and small-fry boys trickle after. I spare a thought for the latter. On a school outing in infant school, a teacher once paired me with a trembling boy led on to the bus when we were already seated. It was his first day of school and he was late. I was only tiny myself but he was as if just calved, wet and tremulously uncertain. I took his hand, sticky with tears and amniotic fluid, and kept it the whole ride.

The time for empathy has passed by the time I encounter the Havelock-to-Blenheim crowd. At Havelock bus stop we wait outside a cake-shop window of unloved standards, including neenish tarts of the hard, bifurcated icing. I never purchase one of these sugary installations, but I am aware of their presence, like a failure of desire, behind the glass. Occasionally in the bus line someone stands back out of sudden country diffidence for the girl in the wrong-coloured uniform. Otherwise, I am one of the last on. Once aboard the scrum crowding the aisle maintains a delusion of primacy by heckling and shoving the hour-long ride. No one takes the empty space next to me. That is, until May Bryant does.

Long, assertive legs, blue plaid uniform slashed to mini, roots and hoop earrings, nails bitten to polished quick. May Bryant. The punctum in this familiar picture of tough/fast is her cleft lip. May lives amidst a monotony of green paddocks the other side of the Canvastown highway, where her Dad works as a farm hand. Without so much as looking their way May irresistibly commands the respect of the man-shaped boys. Flattered by her selection of the worn seat leather next to me, I soak in her vision of slouchy sexuality. We don't talk, exactly, but there is a frisson in sitting together so we keep it up. Somewhere along the line, I realise that she is vulnerable and at least as nervous as me, and I like her even more.

5A

At Marlborough Girls' I have landed in the fifth-form top stream, a place I have never been before and don't even believe in. My previous college was unstreamed; now, here I am disturbing the strenuously guarded academic ranking and, in the process, the equilibrium of my new classmates. I've never cared to know exactly where I stand in the class; I know enough to know the concept is ugly, and that ranking is a dehumanising obsession. And yet, in the seventy-eight-percent mark in home-form English that I am randomly allocated at Marlborough Girls' College, I feel the powers-that-be putting me in my place. I am more competitive than I admit.

Within days of being there I discover that snooty 5A is not a club I wish to be a member of. The feeling is mutual. I am immediately assigned the nickname *Hippy Trippy*. It rankles. I have always been pretty alert.

Hippy is a troublesome term. Few of my father's friends refer to themselves in this way. More often others use the term as a form of denigration. Among Canvastown locals *The Hippy House* has been a by-word for the Floodhouse since my father moved in. If he sometimes deploys *hippy* to self-describe, the word is shaded with irony and self-deprecation. New Zealand hippies of this era are keen to distance themselves from the long Haight–Ashbury shadow and its cultural jargon. Nor, like my mother, is my father given to group membership of any kind. Sometimes his artist friends refer to themselves as *freaks* but this doesn't take either. Like *hippies*, and *beatniks* before it, *freaks* is an import that doesn't correlate with local conditions. I reach for the term *hippy* here because I cannot find a better one.

In 5A I share small talk with the other seventy-percenters, those girls who, unlikely to climb into the starrily oppressive heights of the eighties and nineties, have internalised their lower status and are therefore friendlier. But not much. The snobbery of the ranking system is sufficiently ingrained that it functions to subtly keep each of us apart and trivialise all.

In the typing stream on her way to flunking, May Bryant

seems to neither care nor hold my position in 5A against me. Despite the apparent gulf—I'm also roughly ten inches shorter than her—we recognise each other in the way that shy, scornful people do. And although we don't gossip or confide, abruptly the bus ride is easier and more thrillingly downbeat. This dreary moment followed by this dreary moment followed by this dreary moment, each subcutaneously enlivened by the charismatic insult that is May Bryant.

The silence

Out of the corner of my eye, without quite admitting it, I keep watch for a letter from Grandmother Margaret. At Doreen's Post Office, filed between the Canvastown General Store and the Trout Hotel, mail for the locals is clasped by rubber band and shunted into open wooden cubbies our side of the counter.

Doreen, the dry-mannered countrywoman responsible, conducts all over-the-counter transactions with the poker face of one who knows much about the private lives of her customers. She and I barely exchange a glance, until she turns up in my father's dream diary, where I have trespassed on an idle, school-less afternoon. After my stolen read, I regard Doreen speculatively and with consternation. She's elderly and yet, in my father's eyes, still sexual. I have a hunch there is something disturbingly apt in his fantasies about the woman who commands this wall of apertures: the object of our collective yearning. I feel queasy about entering the premises—but I am the mail hawk.

My father's yield continues to be bare of Margaret's cursive hand. Instead, I receive letters from my best friend, Ingrid, and from a shy first-fifteener who thinks there might be something between us. *Mr Right*, my grandmother dubbed Richard shortly before I left, thereby sealing his fate in my eyes as *Mr Wrong*. I don't reply to his letter for social sorrow. And for Ingrid I find it impossible to translate life on the other side of the looking glass.

Our friendship, begun at Wellington Girls' College, has been for doing, making and being rather than explaining. For perfecting our grasp of twig placement in the watercolours of birds that we paint as we sit side by side. For contracting grass rash from lying in the thigh-high weeds of the empty block a few houses along from hers. For mixing chocolate Quik in the cool of her parents' untended pantry, her mother—sympatico, girlishly large, afloat with medication—in a less-visited bedroom down the hall. If I can no longer share these core things with Ingrid there does not seem any point in staying in touch.

I am brooding on my grandmother. I see her vocalising to Edith Piaf, *Non, je ne regrette rien*, tea towel swirling joyously in hand as she sways across the living room until even the ill-tempered Persian ginger, Mrs Goodcat, regrets not dancing. I hear the yellow enamel Swedish coffee pot murmuring on the stovetop. No one takes cardamom-infused coffee served with whipped cream in Canvastown in 1978—at least that I know of.

Margaret's print takes up most of the real estate on an envelope that doesn't come. In optimistic scale, her hand is more like her daughter's than either cares to acknowledge. What would Margaret say, anyway? *My mistake. Come home.*

If I cannot formulate the words, those aching units of raw between us, neither can she. How I miss and hate her too.

The word

A long letter comes, instead, from a girl whom I recognise and admire as irrepressibly intellectual. Our friendship has been close but without routine except for those imposed by being in the same form class for three years. Now, her letter comes. A goodbye disguised as a hello.

Sandra Butt has an incipient black moustache on skin so pale it takes on eau-de-Nil shades in certain lights, shaggy shoulder-length hair. Just when you are thinking she looks interestingly mannish you catch sight of her wasp waist. Actually, I couldn't give a toss what Sandra Butt looks like. Flowering out of chocolate shagpile, TV dinners and Casey Kasem's Top 40, it is her zany brilliance that commands. She is addicted to commercial radio and can impersonate station insignias, jingles, sound effects and absurdly deep-voiced jocks on demand. She's too cerebral to be one of the art kids, but I watch with envy one afternoon as she goes into a kind of dabbler's trance, creating an effortlessly sci-fi desert with sponge washes and *sfumato* effects, featuring purple cacti, fawn tumbleweeds and green-tinctured skies. She tacks the result on the art-room wall with modest detachment, as if the landscape happened on its own and she was merely an attentive bystander. And yet of all the paintings tacked up only Sandra's is unmistakeably Sandra's.

An ad hoc student of pop culture—everything ordinary and assumed is fodder for her textual reading—she might well have hailed as much from the Birmingham School of Cultural Studies as the basement bedroom of a Tawa split-level. I admire her fiercely, and not only because she gives the lie to so many of my family's certainties.

*

In the first and last letter she ever sends me Sandra writes that of all the people she knows I have *integrity.* I read this bit a few times. It seems to be a cumulative impression rather than attached to any particular event. She is gracious. The first time I stayed overnight at her family home I had to go home early. The self-saucing dinner in foil compartments and Popsicle dessert, the wall-to-wall orange and brown, Sandra's singalongs to 'Rich Girl' and 'Hotel California' disoriented me. The Butts were New Zealanders in American drag. At least, Sandra was. That was the point. She was a meta-pop goddess, but my stomach hurt. I had become homesick for Granny's pensioner flat, the walls hung with modernist prints torn out of art books, and her home-cooked meals. I'd never experienced a subdivision in all its denatured newness before. Even if the place had grown Sandra, I couldn't wait to get out.

Integrity. The word has a completeness I hope to live up to and fear I won't. Even so, Sandra's is one of those rare compliments I am unable to flick off. I have never doubted Sandra's word before. Do I write back? In the perverse way of the heart, the letter means too much to reply to. Sandra Butt is a dropped stitch in time. Unrecoverable.

Agency

By the time I arrive at my father's Floodhouse I am a dedicated over-interpreter of others. In the micro signs of mood and behaviour, their shifting sands, I construct stories. Often, these are stories against myself. I do not express separation anxiety from all that my life at 46A held so much as remain on guard for signs of tension that might precede another break-up. I know that cool spots, even in a lake of warm feeling, can quickly lower the overall temperature.

My father has only this to say about my regrets: I have outgrown life with Grandmother Margaret. He does not think that I have been rejected. In his opinion I provoked my own exit. This he respects, for he sees my leaving, and the unconscious style in which he holds I engineered it, as the gaining of agency. This is salient information and I take it in, a torn-off tatter of adult wisdom from the mysterious volume of self. Not comforting, exactly, but contrary as all self-knowledge is.

Will I get too big for life at the Floodhouse? An anxious thought.

John of Saratoga

Returning from school one dusk I find John of Saratoga cleaving to the ancient rolled sofa arm, ankles crossed, the soles of his long feet black with road filth. The stranger's gaunt draws what light makes it through the clouds of smoke that billow from the wood range as my father rattles its chimerical damper and curses. He is preparing a combination of the usual soya bean omelette and garlicky salad, and fresh peppermint tea in a heavy-spouted teapot. Potatoes, sliced into rounds in the cast iron frying pan, are doused with cream and dusted with paprika before being shoved in the oven in honour of the visitor. My sister has taken the opposing arm and is reading *The Blue Fairy Book*. Coming through the door I am magnetised by the dark-hued human buoy bobbing up the other end of our unstable sofa.

I quickly establish that John of Saratoga doesn't speak much but comes to warm himself in my father's sooty kitchen where the most recent flood-line stains the timber interior a metre up the wall, his utterance upstaged in equal parts by extreme diffidence, an ever-ready irony that operates at his own expense, and a hacking cough. From what I can tell, he is a wanderer seeking the next crash pad, the next hospitably expiring couch whose subsidence draws polite New Zealand bodies towards the vertiginous ditch in its centre. He favours broken-down Salvation Army coats, which enhance his concavity; is dark-haired, nicotine-fingered and carries a dog-eared physics text in his coat pocket. Everything about him tea- and tar-coloured, right down to his teeth, he is like a deteriorated relation of my first love, Cold Tea & Coat.

Mundane biographical details are disdained in the hippy world, direct questions frowned on. When, in *Easy Rider*, Dennis Hopper insistently asks a fellow traveller where he is from, and is just as insistently deflected, self-conscious credo is elevated to taboo. From my father, who thinks *Easy Rider* macho and silly, I learn that John's medieval-sounding nickname is derived from a tiny fishing settlement deep in the Pelorus Sound, where he is based, and that in a former life he was an engineer who migrated from Darwin.

I learn from Dee, from whom my father subleases the Floodhouse, that John of Saratoga periodically goes missing from the hippy circuit. Then, more often than not, his breathing situation will have reached crisis and he is, eventually, to be found in intensive care. Despite being acutely asthmatic, he is known to sleep in a damp swag by the side of the road. That is the sum of available facts. Whoever wrote that romance thrives on an economy of scarcity might have been thinking of Saratoga John.

Despite my school uniform, white socks at half-mast and

puppy fat, I have a taste for suffering and a disdain for lifestyle. A chronic asthmatic smoking himself to death, *how stylish.* My eschewal of the lifestyle category is fortunate because my father's dump is off the dilapidation chart. The kitchen doesn't even sport a tea towel, just a stub of bath towel ingrained with stove grime.

Although she is in the process of setting up house with her lover, Dee maintains the best room in the Floodhouse as hers, visiting it but rarely. This is the light-flooded front room in which I camp on first arrival before reluctantly moving across the hall to its darker sister. Originally, my father and this statuesque potter with serious drapes of gold hair thought they might build a kiln together and share firings. They soon revealed themselves ill suited: Dee accustomed to homage; my father disinclined to render. When their collaboration failed to take my father ended up sub-leasing the house instead.

In Dee's room I can lie in bed and see chinks of cornflower-blue sky or occasionally a star between the wide unlined boards of the walls. Here and there tufts of rose-trellised wallpaper cling like relics of a more couth former life. Blue perforations and chilling draughts acclimatised to, the room is a space in which to brood on the unexpounded facts of my new life, of which there are many.

Sometimes John of Saratoga honours us with a solo visit. Sometimes he turns up in a small party of the Manaroans, commune-dwellers from the remote Pelorus Sound. Once, John of Saratoga arrives accompanied by Eddie Fox, a flashily handsome Welshman, both mounted on Lenny the Horse. My father dreads—and embraces—every option. *Fuck. Visitors!* And he's off in a spin about the catering. *More mouths to feed! What will the horse eat, fuckit?* On the subject of John my father pronounces, with depressive savour, *He's just waiting for death to come along and knock him on the head.*

Personally, I think John of Saratoga looks like a woodcut, or one of those linocuts that are a feature of school curriculum art in the sixties and seventies—only made with graver intent. Hacked out by trowel, ink in deep-cut grooves, graven. It is clear to me that none of it would come together without the cheekbones.

His visits, in reality few and far from forthcoming, are enlarged by my inner saucer-eye, my teen-sorcerer eye. I attribute the magic to John of Saratoga, of course. And I am half right. He is a beautiful riddle modestly stalking the highways of our island. It helps that in my father's house I am inoculated against boys my own age, barely exposed—unless you count the shy, bombastic clods on the school bus, which I don't.

Weather event

The locals call our house *The Hippy House*, which strikes me as inept and inaccurate code for goings-on. For orgies and bong haze and other phenomena that some in the Wakamarina Valley clearly perceive their lives to be deficient in. They have no idea how lacking our household is in the most basic stimulants—television, Coca-Cola, instant coffee, white sugar—let alone opportunistic sex parties. Don't they realise my father is a puritan? Pooling our isolation in the wooden house propped unsteadily on five-o'clock-shadow lawn, abstaining from mainstream entertainments, it is just the three of us, alone together again.

Then, an explosion of hooves around the bend in the valley road: *The Manaroans!* Come to break their journey north or south at my father's, they arrive by collective noun: by horse-drawn hoop and canvas wagon as if directly out of a Western or Eastern European saga; by power of thumb, in ones or twos; or solitary by steed. But, however the Manaroans arrive the air is charged as it is right before an extreme weather event. A weather event inside and outside my head.

Eddie Fox

There are no photographs of Eddie Fox that I know of. I point my borrowed school camera at him once, but he shows his teeth in warning smile and says that tribal people are correct, *a photograph steals your soul.* I shoot him with my camera-eye instead. A few of those likenesses survive here.

Eddie Fox walks on the balls of bare high-arched feet, wearing band trousers caught with rope at the waist, a thick red stripe down the profile of each leg.

The whites of his eyes flash like an animal's on high alert. A whinnying laugh does nothing to dispel the impression. Eddie prides himself on his vigilance, approaching his surrounds with the mystic outlook and deliberate movements of a well-disciplined paranoid.

A gallant who doesn't like other people all that much. Welsh but black Irish in looks. Central casting for gypsy. Did I mention the limp?

*

Not long after Saratoga John has ghosted through, I encounter Eddie Fox in the shadowlands of the hallway. He has come to break the journey from Tahuna, a commune on the outskirts of Nelson, to Manaroa; to rest and graze the chestnut horse he rode in on this afternoon. At my father's suggestion, Eddie Fox follows me back down the hall to build a fire in the front-room hearth.

Eddie preaches the pyramid technique, screwing each sheet of newspaper into a twist, then stacking the kindling into a meticulous tepee so that oxygen can circulate and fan the flames. I look on, interjecting with the occasional question. Eddie reciprocates. In this way, as the fire is ritually constructed so is my arrival at my father's house and the raw acts leading up to this event. If no one has taken such an interest in my history—or my vocabulary—up until now, that's probably because he's earnest as an adolescent, Eddie Fox. A bit Socratic. Perhaps my account of leaving 46A touches some childhood leave-taking or other out-casting of his own. He's just the kind who might have run away to the circus or the sea or to join the military.

As for my father, Eddie Fox gets his goat. *Ah bullshit*, I hear him think as the limping alpha splits a pile of kindling in competitive seconds but fails to help with the dishes or clear his drained mug from the sofa arm. The Welshman is so reliably doctrinaire that my father—physically approximate always, not given to rhetoric or showmanship—is reliably provoked. Perhaps autodidact Eddie reminds him of his didactic dad. He keeps his distaste to himself as best he can. Hippy hospitality is sacred.

For his part, Eddie Fox is not as obtuse as my father believes. Soon enough he finds an excuse to drift out into the overrun garden to check on the horse and the aromal night; mine is the apple for Lenny the Horse with which I follow.

The visual drama of the visitor goes conspicuously unheeded by father and youngest daughter. Young and un-pheromone-clouded, my sister is too haughty to be interested in such a male display bird. She glides by, eyelashes lowered, definitive chin tilted. Distant royalty on the move.

No matter. Eddie Fox and I develop a friendship of sorts: unlikely, provisional, no-strings, Q-and-A-sustained, underwritten by the amusing prospect of what the other will do or say next. By Eddie's deliberation and my impulse. By our mutual verbal pomp and swagger.

Thanks to Eddie, to this day I can nurse a fire through the rickety stages where infant mortality is high, through blustery, smoky adolescence and into full flagrance.

The great beauty

Dressed in a dirty, earth-coloured calico dress that emphasises her fertility-goddess figure, Claire has fox-sharp features and a prominent beauty spot on her cheek. At twenty-one she is younger by six or seven years than the average Manaroan. Regardless, the commune's survival turns on this formidable character.

On her occasional visits to my father's house Claire doesn't say much. Rather, she pulls on a rollie, drinks strong tea out of a blue-lipped enamel mug, chops firewood as well as any man, neglects her beauty in a way that is commanding, and watches whatever there is to go down, go down. Sometimes she chews the end of her thumb, a rare reminder of her youth. *Nail biter*, she confesses, blushing to the root when she catches me watching.

Claire quit school as a teenager. Not long after, she became the gardener–founder of the Manaroa commune. Now she works like a pioneer and smokes like a narrow-eyed cowboy; the New Zealand light is strong. Everyone is a little afraid of her.

Manaroa's bountiful kitchen garden is legendary. I hear of it long before I clap eyes. Its great horticultural beauty is mostly down to Claire and those who tread her green-sprung footsteps: Kate, Sylvie and Bernadette. The garden is given over to herbs, giant rows of salad food and companion plants: frilly kale decades before it has entered urban-hipster consciousness, purple-skinned garlic, the dark-veined beet leaves that make the contents of our salad bowls pithy, marigold and borage flowers for bug-repelling and for eating, and, here and there, a lemon or tamarillo tree. This does not come close to describing the garden's unmarshalled abundance nor its flowers.

It is in the Manaroa garden that I discover those idiosyncratic flowers that resemble two-tone jester hats, aquilegias or—as Kate, herself as leggy and astringent as a spring onion, informs me—*Columbine* after Harlequin's sweetheart. *Aquilegia*. The word is at least half the attraction. *Love-in-a-mist*, with whiskery fronds that screen and frame a single star-shaped blue flower, is another literary siren with an ingenious face. From this time on, I cultivate these mercurial flowers and they me.

Affinities

Kate arrives at the Floodhouse in the company of Claire: one loquacious, the other steadfastly reluctant to be drawn. Everything about them—from their muddy work boots beneath ragged hems to their labour-dented limbs—spells can-do. Kate is directly acquainted with the second wave of American feminism. It might have been she who inspired my father to mail *Our Bodies, Ourselves*, with its black-and-white shots of self-empowering pocket mirror held to labia, for my fourteenth birthday. Secret images right out there in the open that burn a hole in my mind.

In fact, my father has an affinity for the women's movement that predates his acquaintance with Kate. This alliance is not disinterested. Ever since he was born, and thus subjected to the iron law of his headmaster father, my father has found men, and their delusion of entitlement and expertise, an intolerable bore. Decades before *mansplaining* is coined, in another century, in one or other of the departure lounges that criss-cross my childhood, my father fills the time before take-off by pointing out a male stranger gratuitously explaining something to a long-suffering woman over airport coffee.

But Kate. Newcomer Kate's commentaries are so commenting, her puncturing eye so visibly at work, that I retreat into failure to communicate. As for my sister, she emerges from her moody composure, steadies her Wedgwood gaze and indulges in a chattiness I have not seen before. She seems to instantly apprehend Kate's brainy flow of reference and reflexivity. In turn, my sister's drawings of other, less empirical empires; her collection of hand-stitched, over-stuffed, long-nosed velvet *woozles;* and her purloined recipes for bitter medieval lollies, are given due regard by the visitor. Disinclined to join the fun and, frankly, unqualified, I watch the way the tallest and the tiniest make my father's kitchen their scornful salon.

Sylvie

Sylvie has a crystal-cut upper lip and blue eyes that clash symphonically with her hennaed hair. Her high, flirtatious laugh is uneasy in its own skin like an undecided party girl or a horse about to shy. In her late thirties, with soft Norwich vowels, Sylvie is the oldest and most striking of the Manaroans. She is also the one my father feels hopeful about.

I, too, look to this Englishwoman for clues. She is mother-age and voluptuous-bodied—a confusion of signifier with signified, this, for there is nothing especially maternal about Sylvie. Still, she pays me respectful attention on her sporadic visits to the Floodhouse. She and my father are having the kind of vacillating, experimental affair that soon peters to friendship. Butter-skinned, sensible and sometimes a little self-hating, Sylvie is hard to get to know, and I sense this extends to her relationship with herself. Perhaps this shifting opacity drives her interest in the drier, more punishing branches of esoteric mysticism and astrology.

A few years on, when she is on her way out of the hippy world, this handsome woman tells me she wants only *not* to be noticed. Around this time Sylvie becomes strategically interested in the drabbest, most suburban of clothes. She seeks out sensibly cut beige and brown, and lets the henna fade from her hair. Her new disguise throws retrospective confusion on the old. It is strange to see Sylvie's grace so wilfully doused but, as she represents it, she's had it with hippy men. She has recognised that the sexual revolution and its hippy offshoot, the myth of free love without acknowledgement of emotional need or commitment, serves its male proponents first and foremost.

Eventually Sylvie marries a sheep farmer pocketed in the most conservative reaches of the Marlborough Sounds, whose dying wife she has professionally nursed over long years. Immured in this long-duration service, then courtship, Sylvie disappears from the public eye and the feral dreaming of her once flamboyantly communal life at Manaroa.

But when I know Sylvie, when her membership of the back-to-the-land scene is in full swing, she tells me that if you are horny *or* frustrated or simply need to attract a man for sex you might dab vagina juice behind your ear. This is delivered in Sylvie's habitual tone of enlightened neutrality so it is impossible to tell if she has ever done so herself. I am living in Nelson, putting myself through a final year of school, and Sylvie and I are lying companionably in my share-flat bed when she passes this piece of feral arcana on. I stash it. I am lonely but not that lonely, I decide.

In passing

Then there is Suzie. Just once there is Suzie.

She rides up on the back of Lenny, her arms around Eddie Fox's waist. A woman with a face veil made of soiled black lace. Part Māori, perhaps, with unruly black hair, she wears an ancient biker jacket, oversized men's jeans cinched in with a belt, and work boots. I listen out for the visitor's rough voice, but she is mostly at pains to merge with the sputter of male small talk circling with the passing joint. That she is one of those women for whom men count most is apparent. Women always recognise such women. My attempts to categorise Suzie, however, fit about as well as her jeans. She is a statement but one I cannot read.

I try not to watch as Suzie feeds morsels of the evening meal behind the veil. Despite her efforts to merge, the bravado of her costume sets her apart. I am perversely envious of her veil, and of her liaison with Eddie. *Is she Eddie's girlfriend?*

One of the men shrugs off my naiveté. *She's just passing through.*

Increasingly familiar with hippy stonewalling, I persevere and am rewarded. The origin of Suzie's veil is a house fire. *A house fire.* Intimations flicker of a life in wild flux, a life lived harder than many of the itinerants I have met so far.

Interesting tragedy notwithstanding, I decide Suzie is a poseur. The counter culture is full of poseurs, even I know this, though where you draw the line in a society that runs on dress-ups and self-reinvention, I don't consider. Even so, Suzie is like Emily Dickinson's circus. Although it has passed, still you feel the red in your mind.

Hairdressing

The morning after a group of Manaroans arrive I enter the kitchen and another century in the process.

Someone sits on the sofa while another parks on the lino and leans back into the other's knees. With sleepy murmurs or in silence, the first plaits the hair of the second. Both men and women participate for long hair is omnipresent. Not my father, who has shoulder-skimming hair light as a pixie's, and who finds the casual display of tenderness confronting. Lonely as we are for touch in the Floodhouse, the spectacle of so much everyday intimacy is as hard to bear as it is to resist. Softly clattering dishes, my father staves off the allure.

But if Kate is visiting, my little sister, who has a swathe of thick, dark hair, lends her small pointy Venus hands to the action. She is pleased to be released from the artless hairdos our father renders before school each morning and into a woman's care.

Thinking my constant thoughts about *who* wants *whom*, I watch the handiwork unfold from the discrete unit of the unravelling wicker chair.

One morning Claire beckons me over. I struggle to keep the strands taut as I interweave them, and try not to tug her scalp. It is intimidating and an honour to be invited to braid Claire's hair. Her plait reaches to the small of her back. In my nervousness I feel the process is a bit like grooming the tail of a thoroughbred that, hyper alert to contamination by nerves, might shoot out a back leg if you make a wrong move. In reality, Claire is sanguine.

Once, I witness Eddie Fox offer himself up to Claire's brush. I've seen him smooth his jet hair shiny and flat with one hand and loop a perfunctory band around with the other while on his way out the kitchen door. I thought he would jeer at the communal hairdressing, but Claire works her rough magic.

When John of Saratoga submits his mussed tangle to the rite, Sylvie threatens scissors but negotiates without. Saratoga bobs his crow head and exposes ruins for teeth. Concave as a reed and as sarcastic, Bruce likewise capitulates. The Scotsman is rarely sighted on our sofa. *Stoned Monolith*, a wit has dubbed him in reference to his semi-permanent watch with bong on the Manaroa sofa. Bruce isn't particularly welcome at my father's, and the feeling is obviously mutual.

I plait Doug's cloud of hair once only. A stubble-cheeked man, only four or five years older than me, with attractively padded hands, Doug gives the impression it is embarrassing being such a peach. His country courtesy conversely makes me feel that anything longer than a few basic sentences of conversation is a bit over the top. Doug is the place where sentences go to founder or die or be met with a diffident giggle. Sentences being my family's mainstay, we see far less of Doug than I would like.

The cousins

David brings my cousins Rebecca and Ben south to stay a few nights at the Floodhouse. Ben is my sister's age; Becky and I go way back. My uncle must be anticipating a well-starred, riverside holiday for his children. He may also be making a gesture of solidarity towards his freshly separated brother-in-law and recently expelled niece. A plucky gesture, if so, for these are urban people who like their morning coffee from a plunger, and their evening current affairs over the cask red.

On their arrival, the physical delicacy of my younger cousins throws into relief how grim the river-sluiced deformities of the Floodhouse actually are. Even my aunt and uncle's murder house on the Terrace had a semblance of structural decency that ours does not. In the visitors' fastidious presence, I see my father's house anew. It is one thing to live there, another to have such witnesses.

One day I will find creative nourishment in my father's talent for a mess. The imagination sometimes takes flight if there is nothing too materially demanding to hold it down. It is in one of my father's untidy piles, by the sea, that I first begin to write.

Right now, though, no one can relax.

David assumes a blokey jocularity to assuage the shock. *Jesus, Norm.* My father returns the same, although his bloke act feels more like kindly drag. Fag hanging out of mouth, David proves a decent hand at the wood block too. Aware of him discreetly shepherding his children through this unanticipated slum experience, I appreciate that my uncle is a good sport.

I do not remember what my cousins make of my father's breakfast fixture, soya bean omelette.

I do not remember what they make of dandelion coffee, served from a saucepan so encased in old grounds it looks like a Gaudi then filtered through a sieve the size of a dinner plate.

I do recall that, perched on the wood-smoke-blackened sofa, Rebecca eats more like a bird than ever. That Ben, naturally pale, looks ill in the submarine light. That my childhood playmate whimpers in her sleep from the mattress on the floor alongside my bed, and that, woken, I think only of not having my sleep disturbed again.

I do remember that conversation deserts us. Rebecca is uncharacteristically mute. I have entered an arrangement utterly beyond her ken.

As for what we do, there *is* nothing to do. A day out is a visit to my father's cowshed pottery, which is just a cowshed with the addition of a pottery wheel, some pots and my father's portable disarray. We make coil pots and our hands become inhospitably dry. We are city kids.

Maybe it is a test, Uncle David gently nudging his children's mettle. Maybe he harbours a sneaky admiration for my father's pioneer approximations, his approximate DIY. Maybe he just wants to see how another ex-husband and recent solo dad does it. These possibilities notwithstanding, the visit is mercifully short.

Riverside

The tablecloth of fields pocked with sponge-rolls of hay give way to stone-fruit orchards and berry plantations. My father has seen me onto a Newman's bus bound for a two-week working holiday at Riverside Community. Detaching my face from the glass, I jump down, arms rustling sociably with Indian bangles, and make my way up a meandering private road, asking first this then that passer-by where I might find Rob and Kath's. Founded during the Second World War by Christian pacifists, the Motueka community appears disconcertingly tidy and affluent to my poverty-adjusted eye.

Slung on the spine of a hill, Rob and Kath's cottage looks into the knotty embrace of a crab apple tree. My arrival disturbs Rob and Kath, carrying out domestic chores in the nude, not at all. After they have shown me the small room with single bed where I will sleep, and we have drunk a cup of tea, Rob explains that there is a day of the week set aside for going naked if one feels like it. I affect sangfroid while cleaving to my clothes. As far as I am concerned nudity is a spectator sport. In practise, this celebration of nudity only applies to the young *and* physically gifted (Rob and Kath), or the bold.

I have met Rob Francis before at my father's. Everyone is pleased to encounter this informal ambassador for Riverside. His adzed features and radical lack of hair are partnered with a radiant equanimity. He's a bona fide community spirit. *Very clever man, has no enemies*, is how the Cambodian herbalist I consult in years to come would gloss Rob Francis. With a sense of humour as sceptical as her physique, his partner Kath is even harder to parse. Watching her watch this newcomer in her peripherals, I feel certain I have landed in good hands.

As the afternoon lengthens, Kath's youngest sister, Maree, with whom I will be picking raspberries, drops by. Maree lives down the road with a mother and father the same age as my Howick grandparents. When we become better acquainted, I will find these founding Riverside elders like to hold things up to the light, ethics especially, and turn them ruminatively before returning, peevishly, to the business of their day. This discursive spiritual practice is very different from my grandfather's rigid certainties, my father's stubborn intuition or Grandmother Margaret's felt sense of social injustice. Maybe this is why their considerations strike me as so impressive, and so tedious.

Possible bodies

For fact-finding adolescents, the principal attraction of a visit to the house of Kath and Maree's middle sister, Yvonne, and her doll of a husband is that, in the privacy of their own home, they go naked all week long. Once a week is for amateurs. So, one afternoon Maree and I cut loose early and walk down the highway to encounter Yvonne in her natural habitat.

We find two small boys ripping naked through the garden in Stetsons, a plastic pistol in holster and a hand-hewn bow and arrow apiece. Their beauty of a father coaxes beans to a trellis nearby, also without clothes. Weaponry of any kind is censured on community, but Yvonne tells us that she makes an exception for her sons' play. *Censorship breeds violence*, she explains, as she punches down bread dough in her sinuous, emancipated nudity. She is making loaves to stock the community store, where produce and dry goods are free to members. Perched on a bar stool in the sunlight-mote, open-plan room, I process a scene that is more Sally Mann than Diane Arbus.

Maree and I hang around for an hour or two, taking in the nude philosophy and the domestic science and horticulture show. And what a show it is: implicitly sensual yet strangely uneventful. Even so, we manage to make at least one of the star exhibits uneasy. The especial object of our glances, the faun-like husband, finishes with the bean trellis and disappears.

Back on our own, Maree and I ponder which comes first: pretty bodies that are predisposed to getting undressed or the gradual acquisition of pretty bodies after so many hours untrammelled by clothes. We wonder at the genetic windfall of Yvonne's small breasts and boyish hips. We figure these are preconditions to achieving round-the-clock nudity. With our busting-out busts and curves, Maree and I are certain we don't qualify.

On our way back up the hill, a man in office clothes, fresh from community accounts in the church hall, takes us in. *You've grown. You'd make a fine Botticelli angel*, he tells Maree. His compliment falls between us, bringing its own tension. Botticelli is saccharine, and to be disdained. I look askance at Maree in defiant beige overall, colouring to the roots of her auburn hair. Plump as beautiful, a new and interesting possibility. Does it include me? Probably not. We disdain the accountant's hackneyed observation and move on.

The days mooch by in a state of heightened possibility when Maree and I are together, some of it erotic, much of it vaguely atmospheric: nebulous. In the long afternoons and evenings when we swap berry picking for the greenstone Motueka river and float side by side on our backs, it is seemingly boundless, this possibility. When a dowdy male stranger annotates or makes it explicit, less so.

The Murray cloud

For a matter of weeks, the possible finds incarnation in Murray. It is his vanity that attracts our attention. A fellow summer visitor and berry picker, Murray strolls about in pyjama-like ensembles and wears a banded straw hat on his fastidiously soft mane. Cosmopolitan with an English accent, Murray leavens our scorn with his feline grace. It helps that he leaves a trail of scent. For, although we cannot quite believe this, a draught of sandalwood precedes Murray and then follows in his wake. Our instinct for chase is maddened.

We first come across the Murray cloud when it wafts expensively over the row of raspberry canes where Maree and I are bent picking. After this, tracking Murray by fugitive scent alone makes bearable the tedium of afternoons amidst the brambles. Almost nothing passes between Murray and us, but our days improve. Murray is our truffle, and we the truffle hounds. Undoubtedly, he is aware of our hunt. It intensifies his languor.

Eventually, the Murray cloud leads to Eva, a breast-feeding Czech resident on community, with a flawless Snow White visage and a skewering gaze. Murray lives at her house. Are they lovers? Her new baby is not his, but even so. We never get to the bottom of this branch of the Murray mystery. *Gay* doesn't cross our radar. The hippy scene seems incuriously blank on that score.

Family values

With discreet crucifix necklaces, grace before dinner, and the steady train of parental scrutiny on those around the table, the frame of reference at Barb's household is nuclear and holy. Tilting towards the conservative end of the Riverside spectrum, hers is one of the more overtly Christian families I meet. Barb herself is a rangy woman with a gamine haircut, an unyielding expression and the unnerving habit of allowing a silence to stretch before terminating it. Her husband and two boys melt to insignificance beside her.

Once I am seated at her table, Barb observes a period of tacit scrutiny before firing off, over the after-dinner board games, a number of probing questions about my living circumstances and educational prospects. Hers is the kind of cross-examination I have so far avoided. Eager to please, I trip along, uneasily fluent and, as I later learn, wholly unconvincing in the high beam of my host's regard.

When it gets back, Barb's summation is as unsparing as I feared. *She said you were much younger than you appear. And that it was ill advised, being away from home on your own*, reports Maree, relaying the message unadorned so that we can turn over its accuracy or fallacy. Outwardly, I am rebellious. Inwardly, I lose no time cutting straight to the subtext: *fraud.*

Barb has nailed my conundrum and me in the same breath. The aura of bad faith that has begun to creep into my dealings with certain adults closes in. I am younger than I seem, but circumstance requires this seeming of me. Uncomfortable as I feel, as far as I can see there is nothing for me to do but carry on.

After magic hour

Riverside is having a festival, the extravagant rubric for parties in these parts. It is not as downbeat as the ones my father stages in the paddock next door, nor as wild as I might hope. Staunchly well organised—like everything at Riverside—it is more like a festival crossed with an A&P show than a hippy happening. Crafty in a way that draws on Women's Institute sponge cakes and preserves, and featuring beekeeping displays by an apiarist in a bee hat. The A&P craft element is death to me. I go instantly dull-eyed at the prospect. Far more promising are the travellers arriving in converted buses and house trucks or by thumb. Women in gored velvet and pretty single men, and the ubiquitous sannyasins in their saffron pyjamas, wooden beads and anything-goes.

The climactic dance in the church hall that night is a Crosby, Stills, Nash and Young knock-off to which I wear a swirling bat of a thing—a voluminous black op-shop skirt with a border of mountains, spruce and clouds, hand-painted in calligraphic strokes. I team this with a dusted-pink silk square folded in a triangle and tied over my breasts. Scarf boob tubes are the thing. Maree sheds her overalls for a sweetheart-neckline dress, beads and platforms. Later, I find her de-accessorised and radiantly Maree again.

It is packed inside the hall and Maree and I spend the night losing and finding each other, spinning off into separate trajectories. These are her people, and she busies herself with them. I dance and linger. I like the girlish, slightly ascetic young men with marine gazes best. Am I attracted to them because their sexually cool temperature ensures nothing ever happens? Maybe. Keenly aware that I am too young for anyone here—an awareness that can, and does, eventually turn—I intercept undercurrents and looks between others, skim off a vicarious few for myself.

As the night shifts to adult business and my mood with it, I follow the cat's-eyes and sprawling Milky Way down the unsealed highway towards a single bed in the colonial wooden villa given to overflow guests.

Marijuana fumes and murmurs from the post-party huddle of strangers in the next room seep under the bedroom door. I hug the shadowy contours of the roadside room to me, and the anxious voices of self-censure soften. The faint din of the band down the road is like the sea in a shell held to the ear. Peripheral to the action, far enough flung to contemplate it, I am where I want to be for now.

How to be

Wearing the fifty-dollar black-and-magenta dress on which I blew most of the proceeds from berry picking at Riverside, I go about in a cloud of fennel perfume. I don't shave under my armpits, and the sweat that clots there is pungent and sweet. My mother comments on this during a rare visit. She recommends I rub the puce-veined eau de cologne mint, growing wild out back, under my arms. Crushed, the leaves give off a weak odour that is no match for my stink.

My mother's musk, while also falling short of subtle, is more alluring. Oiled from head to foot, hair looped into plaits that make horns above her brow, she smells of the raw leather that she hems her skirts with, and the linseed oil with which she obsessively bastes the mataī floors of her ex-gold-miner's shack five or six miles up the valley from my father's. Those floors will eventually become sticky-dark with over marinating and, then, only reluctantly release the passing soles of inhabitants and visitors. Initially, however, ringed with bright navel oranges loosed from their case—freewheeling decorative flora—the boards gleam from her attentions. Dressed in crushed velvet, hand-cut slits in unexpected places, reflexively edged in giant stitches, my mother gleams too.

In this exceptional visit to the Floodhouse for a viewing of her recently arrived eldest, my mother's shuttered regard takes in my body. *Your breasts are like darts.* Her lover Heinz looks on. I cross my arms and hunch my shoulders into an angry, effacing package. The dress is a fashion-plate rag to my mother's rejection of all things establishment, a classification that migrates from people and practices to a complicity of objects. It has a blouson bodice overhanging a drawstring waist, full sleeves. Cerise blooms float across my breasts. My mother blinks at the ambitious flowers and denounces them *bourgeois*. Perhaps she sees me as the envoy of her mother, Grandmother Margaret, a woman from whom her own teenage separation is an unclosed wound.

Under my mother's regard, my own secret reservations about this peak fashion item come together. Everyone but my father—who gives us his back—looks, blinks, looks again. Conical and upstanding, involuntarily directional: my sudden breasts. Abrupt animal lushness seems to be happening independently of me. I am in the process of being re-bodied with appetites that mock my baby fat and lack of prettiness. How to be this clutch of contradictions? Stranded on the raised step between kitchen and hall, unsure to which zone I belong, I scowl a disappearing silence.

On my mother's side

She has indelibly a painter's eye, my mother. We have recently discovered that her father was a painter too. Thanks to my grandmother's selective (in)discretions, my mother grew up not knowing she was the result of an affair with Patrick Hayman. Not until she was thirty-three did she know the identity of her biological father or, indeed, that there was anything to know.

Five or six generations ago, the Haymans were among the first Jewish families to settle in New Zealand. More recently,

as a young man sent out by his wealthy family to Christchurch from England to manage multiple retail interests, Patrick had proven without aptitude for business. It must have been as he wished. A student of painting, drawing and poetry, a contemporary and friend of Colin McCahon, Patrick settled in Wellington for a few years in the early 1940s.

As Margaret was married when she had the affair with Patrick, my mother's paternity became a further closely kept secret. Margaret had more to lose than Patrick. This did not stop her conceiving four daughters to three different fathers during one enduring marriage. She had a knack for affairs or, looked at another way, she did not. Margaret's husband was an architect who fathered the eldest and youngest daughters, Diana and Melissa, fourteen years apart. The loneliness of that long-distance marathon, her first marriage, must have been ameliorated then intensified by two significant affairs in the middle. Both affairs produced children: first Amanda and then my mother, Christina.

In the backwater of conservative opinion that was New Zealand in the 1950s, my own father knew of my grandmother by reputation long before they met as *The Scarlet Woman of Lower Hutt*. Thanks to this, my father was thrilled to meet his new girlfriend's mother—and intimidated. Ahead of her time and subjugated by it too, Margaret Ferris née Beere must have felt that divorcee status was an even bitterer possibility for a woman than the scarlet designation. Eventually she enjoyed both.

Her second and final marriage was to a recent Hungarian immigrant not much older than her teenage daughters Amanda and Christina. She had one son, Martin, with Elemér when she was forty-four. It was 1960, and late for a woman to be giving birth by the standards of the time. *A sympathy marriage*, Margaret called it. The sympathy was clearly one-sided because she quickly found herself a divorced solo mother on the poverty line. Given the limited choices available to her, this was the choice she made. It was an ill-conceived marriage, but then her volatile new husband was in his early twenties. Still forming.

These are the skerricks of secret history I absorb over the years.

In the last few years of my life at 46A, I engage in blue-leaved aerogram correspondence with my freshly discovered grandfather Patrick, now a mildly famous painter living in Barnes, London. On the evidence of my letters, Patrick thinks I should become a journalist, but he lets nothing slip on the subject of the past, and I do not know to ask. In turn, my grandmother has little to say of Patrick beyond the tart observation that he was *always thinking of his own comfort. A sensualist and selfish*, although she lets slip that she might have run away with him had he asked.

Nearly twenty years later, Margaret's inspiration for my name in Joan Miró, a painter whom Patrick greatly admired, might have induced in him a smile and a pang of—what exactly—regret, nostalgia, relief? She was a woman of great physical and atmospheric loveliness, my grandmother. In reality, Patrick didn't hear of my existence until much later.

My mother says that she had known, intuitively, that she was Jewish since she was a small child and found herself unable to believe that the architect whom she called *Daddy* was her real dad. *My false father*, she retrospectively called, not without affection, the man who tolerantly brought her up. But the nickname that sticks to Gerard Ferris down the years is *Smog*. Aunt Amanda uses it liberally throughout my

childhood too. Did Gerard smoke a pipe? Long departed from my grandmother's life by the time I arrived to live with her, I never met him. At the time of writing, my mother confides that she was thinking of London smog and its way of disguising landscapes, both real and emotional, when she coined the name. Long before she knew what core truths it obscured, an enfolding haze existed between her unidentified stepfather and herself.

The sisters were not the only ones to experience their stepfather's nebulous retreat. Throughout my childhood, my grandmother describes Gerard Ferris as the husband who spent long hours every weekend locked in their beige Ford Prefect, parked outside their house, eating boxes of chocolates. As a child of eight or nine, the subtext concerning Margaret's second husband is not lost on me. This was a man unable to cope with the riotous dance of female life—with all its deceptively pleasing pin-tucks and smocking—inside the family home.

On enquiry my mother, who is usually blind to the details of automotive manufacture, supplies the family car's make and colour. As for the incriminating chocolates, they were, she says, chocolate peanuts with a picture of a woman in glamorous sunglasses on the front of the box. The beige Ford Prefect *was* parked out front, but Smog himself was up on the house roof, which he was supposed to be fixing but where he had instead taken a book and tied himself to the chimney to read undisturbed. Escape artist. She was always the better storyteller, my mother.

Meanwhile, my mother's biological father, Patrick Hayman, returned from Wellington and his affair with my grandmother to his birth city, London, where he married the ballet dancer Ba. Ba as in Barbara, pronounced with a posh *ahhh*.

Decades later, this unknown father and his adult daughter's meeting was not a success. My mother took the trip, in company with her partner Heinz, from Dargaville to Pat and Ba's home in Barnes soon after Margaret offered up unsolicited the name of Christina's *actual* father. Why Margaret chose to do so at that particular moment I do not know but the fact of Patrick must have been an undisclosed ache those previous three decades. Did it feel good to finally out him?

At the London meeting of Christina and Patrick neither was inclined to claim the other nor, almost as importantly, their work—for my mother was a painter by this stage too. It would not have helped that each experienced the other's spouse as unendurable. Heinz's Rosicrucian certainties were not easy for others to swallow. And posh-voiced Ba did not welcome the flagrant reality of Pat's sudden daughter, a living reminder of the infertility of her own marriage. When I picture their meeting, I imagine how the body language of the unrelated women would have stiffened. It is my mother I feel for. She speaks of the wheel of Camembert, a covetable luxury by contemporary Antipodean standards, Patrick kept in his Barnes fridge but did not invite her to share. Into this testimony of gastronomic slight, a world of hurt is compressed.

Patrick died of a heart attack before I could meet him. As I write I can see my own physiognomy in his smooth face and doubting smile, arm protectively at rest across his body as he rests on his southwest London garden bench. Reproduced in black and white in the catalogue for one of his posthumous exhibitions, Patrick Hayman clearly doesn't trust the photographic process.

Looking at his shy, complex regard afloat in a sea of leaves, it occurs to me that his paintings, which often include poems or literary fragments, might have been gardens to him. I sometimes think of this when am writing: that I am making a garden to roam in.

Dirty, decorous

From Sylvie and Jewels I acquire the habit of wearing second-hand forties crêpe de chine and rayon dresses featuring tailored pleats, gores, cloth bows, buttons, belts, and soft collars that remind me of those droopy-faced flowers, violas.

From the Manaroans I learn to treat these exquisite things, which shrink alarmingly and stiffen strangely when washed but resize dry, as all-occasion. I don't think twice about mucking out or composting the garden or fetching buckets of water in unravelling tea or cocktail dresses. Just the thing for rural life with an audience of sheep, cows, horses and hens. Under contour-skimming crêpe you might layer an Indian wraparound skirt to dip in unconscious waves or a saggy, vintage viscose petticoat dyed leaf green. It's cold in these climes. And yet, no knickers. I never see a pair of knickers in all my years in the hippy world, unless they are a pair of post-war, peach cami-knickers hanging on a washing line. And I don't see too many of those. Bras are not even in the lexicon. In the warmer months, breasts are often bare. The Manaroans are poor but disdaining. No one wears jewellery. A shell cross-section collected from the tideline, strung on leather and worn as a choker, serves. In a gesture towards a previous urban incarnation, Kate has a toe ring.

Sylvie's style is emblematic: a bit dirty, a bit decorous. The look, though cultivated, isn't quite as artful as it sounds. The fit might be baggy or clinging, depending on what you happen upon. The skirts are mud-hemmed, holey, faded and end in clay-caked tramping boots, gumboots or, come summer, bare feet stained and spread from walking unshod.

Sylvie introduces me to a Blenheim op shop where the bins are stuffed with the abandoned garments of bygone generations of country society. Rich pickings, literally. I pay ten cents for a navy crêpe dress with gored skirt I find tangled in a couple of gigantic bras. Windows shaded in dust, the op shop is rarely open, but when it is, its empty but for us. Blenheim sees itself as a discreetly respectable town. We see it as unimaginative. No one wishes to be seen in the beautiful cast-offs of the dead and forgotten bar us hippies.

It does not occur to me that another, subliminal source of these inclinations may lie further back, in the depths of my mother's 1940s childhood when so many of these fashions were current. At that time, my mother's relation to these pieces, immaculately stitched and ironed by my grandmother, was ambivalent. There is a story I savour as a child about the day my infant mother jumped not once but twice into the agitator washing machine while it was in operation in first one and then another such dress. Initially just for the hell of it, and then, dried off, told off and smartly dressed again, because the effect on her mother was so sensationally forbidding.

Perhaps my mother is reacting still, for, from her vantage at the top of the Wakamarina Valley, she frowns down on all pretty things. *Mediocre, conventional, middle class.* Setting these words on the page does not do justice to the vitriol with which she wields them, *conformist* their patently loathing subtext.

No matter, the women of my family are all obsessed with clothes, fabric and textiles, a trait that my mother and

I expressly share these days, a constant intelligence we swap back and forth. Now, my mother glosses whatever period dress I have recently come by with detailed notes, relishing the side trip into her and her schoolfriends' past. Wearing a fez fashioned from a snakeskin handbag, a crocheted veil and other garments that she has hand-stitched over and over into a transporting tapestry, she is ever more sartorially playful and elaborate as she ages. On Grandmother Margaret's side, we are descended from French Huguenot silk weavers and seamstresses. On Grandfather Patrick's, secular Russian Jewish scholars. Grandfather Sam's descendants worked in a London candle factory. These are the remainders and scraps of family history in my possession as I write.

Fifteen

From what I can tell, John of Saratoga doesn't have a girlfriend. Not one of the Manaroan women in clay-trimmed gowns and shaggy hand-knits who visit the Floodhouse come with or for John of Saratoga. It appears a solitary-inclining world, the hippy world, even as it gathers our three in its loose embrace. Liaisons are worn lightly. You don't see handholding or passionate public kissing. Amidst the swirl of the group, people hold themselves aloof, even when disappearing off together for the night. Dedicated to keeping the sexual possible alive, this cagey, obscurely low-commitment style of conducting affairs does not admit of emotional need.

Undiscouraged, heavily influenced by Tolkien, I send John of Saratoga an invitation to my fifteenth birthday, hand-painted on the papery white underside of a large rangiora leaf. The broad, painted leaves crisp at the edges as they dry. A few spoil with spots of rot. Enough survive to send out to a guest list that is mainly Manaroan. Saratoga John's is adorned with a tiny white swan squished in around the hand-lettered essentials of time, place, bonfire. I mail it to the Nelson commune, Tahuna, where he was last sighted and where it might reach him one of these days. Phones don't feature in my reckoning. No one has one. At Doreen's Post Office I insert the leaf in the slot provided for more conventionally shaped letters, hoping against hope that it will fall into John of Saratoga's hands.

An endless series of empties ensues: of standing at the window of the front room in case one of the locals merely drives past, of Saratoga John enleafing the branches of thought.

Eventually the day rolls in. My father sets a fire with tree boughs and demolition timber in the paddock adjacent to the house. Inside, my sister toils at horehound toffee, the recipe culled from Culpeper's *Complete Herbal* (1653), a copy of which somehow came to be floating around the Floodhouse and my sister has made her own. Horehound toffee is for colds and sore throats, but she has been ruminating on this particular delicacy ever since I arrived. *Horehound toffee*: the name demands it be brought into being.

I fill my father's dug-up nineteenth-century bottles and Mason jars with weedy bouquets, and anchor wine chenille over the mantel in the parlour, where tamarillos in packing-case coffin, windfall pears, a record player inside its own suitcase, and dust motes in a shaft of greenery-filtered light are the only, lonely players. Undergrowth shoves up against the window. A shiny, two-gallon square tin of cold-extracted liquid honey stands in a corner awaiting my mainlining father. Waiting is my main game too.

Among the first guests to arrive is my father's potter friend Jenny Doole, who has driven from the Wairau Valley with her boyfriend, who presents me with a tiki-faced statue he has carved from wood and topped with a mohawk of teased nylon rope. While thanking him, I leave a hairclip in his ginger beard and fret for the rest of the party over whether to tell him.

John Hadwen, my first friend in Canvastown, a lanky twenty-seven with fast-loping wit to match, climbs out of the minivan—which doubles as a school bus—parked out front. When not weaving at a room-sized loom at his house, John drives the school run. I unscroll his gift in the Floodhouse hall: three women in classical drapery surround an apple tree encircled by a snake, their linked hands at the centre of the frame drawing the viewer's eye into the dance. I don't quite know what to make of the Pre-Raphaelite daughters of Night and Darkness who look out from Edward Burne-Jones's *The Garden of the Hesperides*. I don't wish for John Hadwen to discover that I identify more with Eeyore, the miserabilist donkey in *Winnie-the-Pooh*, than these unreasonably long-legged nymphs.

As evening falls, Saratoga John appears amidst a clot of Manaroans. Humorous and occluded as ever, he arrives bearing the gift of a pot plant. A *pot* plant. Someone brings out a guitar. My father, his suitcase-with-needle. There's milling and dancing in the paddock to Dylan's 'Hurricane' and 'Sara'. Thanks to Bob, my father is on the lookout for a Scorpio sphinx in a calico dress. His local buddy Julie Tait is under the macrocarpas with a drink, maintaining a boisterous, faintly embarrassed presence, brooding about sex or the lack thereof like everyone else. I've never seen this farmer intimidated before, but she'll be the first to admit the

Manaroans have done it. All that unavailable male beauty—and the bullshit that goes with it. *Bullshit* is a word Julie uses expressively and often, a dragnet for diverse, uncomfortable or unjust experiences. I know how she feels.

At its zenith the bonfire signals the drinkers from the Trout Hotel at road's end. These arrive, according to their vocation, drunk. With the appearance of this motley crew, I am encouraged by my father to follow my sister to bed. The paddock party is degenerating into chaos. Farm labourers and hoons throw bottles. The sensible have long departed. Having retired for the night himself, my father has reappeared, a politely indignant human force field in holey long johns, to send the strangers home and the guests to bed.

Older than most of the Manaroans by a decade, my father is uncharacteristically authoritarian when it comes to substance abuse, regular meals and early bedtimes. Often stoned, the Manaroans are, as a rule, too poor to get drunk. A single flagon of Dr John's Cherry Wine, cheap albeit extremely proof, has arrived with them tonight. When my father puts in his reappearance as harried patriarch in improvised pyjamas, people are surprisingly compliant. The hooting locals list into the scented dark like ships in minor distress. The Manaroans drift to bed in the parlour, on the disembowelled sofa, or wherever they can find floor space. I observe this in hummingbird flights from my room for a glass of water, a flutter down the hall to stand in an open doorway to send or catch another goodnight. The important bit is that John of Saratoga has made the minor odyssey to our Floodhouse on the occasion of my fifteenth birthday, bearing a flatteringly inappropriate gift.

Next day, I will plant the seedling in the back garden and inveigle my father into taking a snap of me—in growing-out shaggy-dog haircut, hanging proudly on the spade, my sister assisting—with the minor piece of grey foliage at the bottom of the frame. *I'm not going to jail for a marijuana plant you have no real interest in*, he will exclaim as he rips it out a few hours later. But this bathetic event is yet to come. Right now, I savour the significance of Saratoga John's gesture. For that is what I have, significance in lieu of closer contact.

Signal loss

One day each school week I suffer sudden total energy loss. This is the day I prop in bed or resume my front-window station, in flowered nightie, in case anything moves out on Wakamarina Valley Road. As morning crosses into afternoon, I might wank in the enclosing summer grass of our uncut front lawn. My sister is at school, my father at the pottery cowshed. I am waiting for *White Album*-era George Harrison and stardust to fall.

In reality the only thing that falls is my academic ranking in 5A, sliding several points as I fail to impress form teacher Mr Blakely, the Irish teacher of English, with my absences. Blakely is a bachelor, a status well-established among my classmates, who compete to offer up bouquets of their smarts. I am unused to the speculative pressure of the collective female gaze as it lingeringly objectifies the male teachers. It makes anyone vaguely eligible painfully vain. Blakely is no exception. I sense that in the class's obsession with the form teacher, there is a note of camp, a reflexive and wilfully overdone performance staged for itself. Oh, the voluptuary of the collective swoon. 5A's flirtation with Mr Blakely is a bit like the *Grease* moves sweeping Western civilisation that year.

A gossipy grid of ebulliently orchestrated and ritualised moves reaching for but falling short of ecstasy.

Like me, my school-bus acquaintance May Bryant is only an intermittent user. Unlike me, her days off at least *begin* on the bus. Disembarked, she's off for the day, to smoke and drum up whatever life there is to be had *in that hole, Blenheim*. (Actually, that's my father speaking.) May almost never graces the worn seat leather on the return journey. Most likely she's at the flat of her mechanic boyfriend: multiple car hulks parked on a defoliated lawn; motorbikes in the living room; that awesome flora, a tattoo, efflorescing on his rope-lean upper arm.

With actual *Grease* moves raging in the playground, corridors and school gym ahead of the school social, May, who is rangy in her too-small white shirt with the sleeves rolled at the shoulder, appears a natural to the genre. By now, however, I know her well enough to know she'll spend the school dance smoking outside: tacitly commenting on the chorus-line within. I will be attending the social thanks to 5A Class Representative Nerissa, who has clocked my busing situation and invited me to sleep over. Nerissa is a brunette with alert brown eyes, brisk as a bird. Kind.

This is how I come to assemble myself in Nerissa's bedroom on the evening of the dance. There's such expectancy in the way my host severs store tags and smooths herself into strapless blue chiffon with ruched bust and swing skirt, tan nylons and industrial strength foundation. So much tan, so much untroubled identification, so much small-town insider knowledge. For a brief moment I wish I could borrow her baby-blue-and-tan camouflage. Instead, in the room of porcelain figurines, I slip into something that fails to register the fifties theme and, naive of make-up, am done. I am going to the ball off-theme but with a germ of unkillable hope.

On our way in and then out of the event, I glimpse May dressed in a truckload of mascara and something fuck-you. She's hanging on the asphalt with a couple of unfamiliar older boys. What else? Acknowledgement by May Bryant briefly hikes my status and dispenses a welcome jolt in an otherwise uneventful night. Inside the Marlborough Boys' school hall, dowdy in mufti, we of 5A discover that our *Grease* moves have already reached their apotheosis in the Marlborough Girls' gym. Our well-rehearsed routine peels off into chaos and misstep as shared rhythmic objectives come adrift on the hard-to-judge current of boys. The dance floor honours its own, and we are not they.

On return, Nerissa's manicured suburban home only extends the anticlimax. We are nice about it, but it is obvious to both of us that our friendship, conceived in charitable intention and civic goodwill, will not take.

Strange, brilliant

John Hadwen briefly played guitar in Split Ends before they substituted the closing *ds* for *z* and found fame as Split Enz. His must have been an ad hoc stint in the band's pre-history, as John Hadwen's name no longer appears in the records. During those short-lived days he painted his student bedroom black, floor and ceiling inclusive, so that he slept and woke in a floating world, paintings swimming trippily to meet his eye. He was an art school student. It was the early seventies. Now he is a professional weaver who drives the afternoon shift of the school bus run from Havelock to the Trout Hotel. His wife, Sue, takes the morning.

When I board this vehicle outside the Shop of Depressed Cakes on Havelock's main road for the return trip, John acts like a demented outtake from *Country Calendar. Gidday! Have a good day at the office, sheila?* Just in case I don't get the satire, John leers and winks in the rear-vision mirror as I make my way to the door. It helps that, folded into the driver's seat, John's is one of those asexual builds, limber and nerdy as a pipe cleaner. His oversized gesture is endearing; it could so easily land badly. I wonder what the other kids think, but one glance establishes how benumbed they are by bus ride number two or three and the prospect of mucking out then homework to come. I practise not smiling at the cows the rest of the way home, along the valley road on foot. When John pings his whiplash smile at me again next day, I capitulate on sight.

Sue Hadwen took my father under her wing when she first encountered him as the only dad at Havelock playgroup. Their friendship outlived his marriage. It is Sue who, having witnessed firsthand the Floodhouse's ground-zero plumbing, extends the invitation to me, newly arrived from the city, to take a bath once a week at theirs. If Sue imagines my facilities shock to be acute, she is right.

Sue and John have actual running water in a tidy wooden house set on a moat of lawn behind a hedge along the Canvastown highway. Staying on the school bus in order to bathe at the bus driver's after school, a freshly Vimmed bath with a yellow rubber duckie, and an actual electric bulb glowering in the socket overhead become my routine. After bath hour John plays me Steely Dan, Joni Mitchell and Charles Mingus records, and takes the piss out of my hippy father. He doesn't really believe in hippies. Hippies make him worry about their kids.

The air is warm and linty in John's studio. It is like being invited underground, under the root structure of some vast tree. Giant loops of coarse earth-coloured yarn are anchored to the wall. John crouches beneath at the loom, eyes rimmed red from conjunctivitis and over-concentration, hands in constant motion. He seems to like me there, perched on the edge of industry, as he ducks the shuttle under the giant frame's lacings to the sound of *The Hissing of Summer Lawns.*

It is with John that I smoke my first joint and confuse his moustache with a mouse. I stay pretty straight, actually, and ad lib the rest. I must be convincing for John and Sue insist I stay over on the sofa. Awakened by soft cries in the night, I creep down the hall past the warp and weft of giant limbs and trunks that extrude from one of John's corporate-lobby-size woven hangings, *Confluence I, II* or *III.* Other confluences hog my attention. The sounds of John and Sue making love waft through their open bedroom door. I hover, absorbing acoustic proof that I am not the centre of the universe or, more importantly, John's universe. Somehow, my belief that we are soul mates goes undented.

One evening after school John reaches down his acoustic guitar from the wall and sings me a song in a reedy voice. It's not very strong this voice. If only I were older. If only there were no brisk, kind, sensual Sue. Not pausing in his shuttle-stitch, John finishes and says, *Your life must feel like shit right now. But although you may not believe this, it's going to get better.* And because it does feel like shit—ejection from my grandmother's followed by crash-landing at my father's appalling crash pad—and because John asserts it so in his sinusy alto, his face drained of lampoon, I do believe it. I am freshly bathed, after all.

In the cherry orchard

My father has produced a pup tent. Thanks to this I am able to accept an invitation to join the Manaroans for the seasonal cherry pick. It is the last days of the Floodhouse. I go unchaperoned.

In the grassy-floored Blenheim orchard, hours of climbing ladders to pluck and then pitch the black fruit to buckets waiting below are diffused by daydream. The dappled sunlight encourages drift and, answerable to none, my cherry yield is as shallow as my pay. Having no real need of money yet I am a dilettante when it comes to hard work and its monotonies. My real concern is the incomprehensible social code of nights around the fire: conversation, joints and Dr John's Cherry Wine. My silence is an incompetence that I feel fiercely. Even worse are my compensatory impulses.

On the second night, the fireside talk turns to ancestry. After a stoned comparison of notes, one of the men sneers, *We're all mongrels anyway.*

Everyone agrees.

Is it the tone or the clubby populism that makes me haughty? *I'm not a mongrel!* I've said it before I know it. Silence spreads around the campfire. I've spurned the contrarian egalitarian impulse. Who do I think I am?

This faux pas sets me on the even more impulsive course of winning back the warmth of the speaker, Curly. In Curly there is nothing of the vestigial girlish beauty that velvets many of the young hippy men I've met so far. Later, I will learn that Curly actually lives on the Graham Downs commune, where he dosses down in a large, tarp-covered hole in the ground. I don't know this yet, however. All I have really noticed is his constant laugh, mistaking it for popularity, and he my need for acceptance.

The advantage is Curly's and he takes it.

The action inside my borrowed pup tent that night is swift, non-considering and unrelated to pleasure. I've never had sex before. No sooner has Curly finished than he pulls aside the tent flap and ejects a *woohoo!* into the night. If the painfully abrupt style of penetration hadn't alerted me, the insight is irresistible now: *I am a conquest.*

Contempt for Curly almost restores me. I don't believe in virginity. I think it medieval. I think *this man* is medieval. And not in a good way, like Culpeper's horehound toffee or John of Saratoga's name. For my part, I realise I have been in a hurry to lose this thing, this *virginity.* I think I will not speak of what has occurred—or of Curly—to anyone. They are *unspeakable.*

It is Sally Everett, herself the mother of a young daughter, who takes me aside to broach the subject of unwelcome attentions, and of natural birth control, next morning. Curly practised withdrawal, a method Sally practises reasonable doubt concerning. She thinks Curly is fatuous and maybe worse but, after a short drubbing, she curbs her tongue. On the subject of natural birth control, she is more expansive. There is a popular text outlining the rhythm method that is almost a bible in hippy circles. Eventually I will come by a copy of it, and a thermometer. After incomplete absorption I will treat this text as the contraceptive itself—rather than the intensive programme it sets down of observation, vaginal temperature charting and abstinence during fertility. But this is later, and those days of imperfect science will be, by definition, short-lived.

Sally's practical intervention in my sex education makes her unusual in these parts. For her vigilance and her curt denouncements, I am equal parts gratitude and avoidance. There is shame and inexperience at work, and I am jealous of my autonomy too, especially in relation to the wrong people.

River gods

At the Floodhouse there are more elemental troubles to consider. After a short, violent spate of rain, the Wakamarina is on the rise. The elemental is about to reassert its unsparing primacy in our lives.

In our gumboots and oilskins, my sister and I hand cartons of books and a few personal effects to my father, who, balancing on a sideboard, hoists them into a manhole in the ceiling. This improvised arrangement is stoppered with a kapok mattress, which flops halfway out like an outsize huhu grub. My father props the other mattresses on top of the furniture, which is, in turn, abandoned to the anticipated floodwaters. The kitchen utensils and crockery will have to go it alone—may even float off over the aqueous lino with a runcible spoon.

I am indignant about my father's lack of a plan, but hardly surprised. As far as I am concerned, the house already belongs to the river gods. Joey the cat must agree for, to my sister's grief, she is nowhere to be found. My father is less concerned. Joey came to us as a stray and has always ebbed and flowed according to her own tides.

We wait in the Volkswagen for our cursing father, school bags stuffed with clothes slung across our bodies. My sister is accompanied by a selection of soft toys that includes a long-snouted woozle, while I hug the pink sateen quilt from the days of 46A. My father drops me at John and Sue's to spend the night on their sofa. The Hadwen's rent their cottage, formerly the farm's original homestead, from Julie and Alan Tait across the paddock. That is where my father and sister are going—to bed down in the Tait's low-slung farmhouse in rooms lightly infused with mutton and sausage fat.

Julie and Alan Tait extended the hand of friendship when my father and mother first set up house among the insular Canvastown community. The farmers offered the use of land and disused milking sheds, into which my father moved his pottery wheel, and where he built an adjacent brick kiln, rent-free. These days my father sells his wares directly to those who pull up off the highway and are, as he happily notes, of an overwhelmingly female clientele.

The Tait's generosity encompasses my sister and me, who, at various times, have ridden in the saddle of their tolerant old horse Elizabeth as she takes a ponderous step or two around the home paddock between mouthfuls of grass. My sister more than me.

There is a photograph of Paola on Elizabeth, in which she is captured side-on, bareback, holding the reins. A tiny red shoe pokes from a skirt knitted in garter stitch with the ends of different coloured skeins of wool. Mounted high on the heavy white horse—a fact emphasised by the low camera angle and sloping paddock—my sister is smaller than Elizabeth's grazing head. A pithy sense of character radiates from her as she looks down towards the photographer from centre-frame. My father stands off to the side in homespun jersey, washed-out Wranglers and work boots. A man in his early thirties with a certain loose grace, he is not as tired as he thinks he is. My sister and he share wide, light-struck foreheads that draw the eye and make you wonder what each is thinking. There are straw flowers plaited

into Paola's crown, signifying that either she alone or both she *and* my father are still living up the valley with my mother Christina at the time the photograph is taken. These would have been the last days of my parents' marriage or the early ones of their split. Painful, regenerative forces are at work.

My father is close to Julie Tait. Ever vocal about the under-stimulation that is farm life and *this shithole Canvastown*, Julie has recently embarked on a psychology degree by correspondence. Everything she says is loud and exasperated, a verbal assault. No sooner has she parked the Kingswood out front, polyester flowers warping across her bulk as she wades through our lawn in the breathless time of extra-large people, than I will hear her exclaim, *Shit Norm!* and she'll be off, winding him up. She loves nothing better than to talk emotions with the subsistence guy down the road, my father.

At the Tait's tonight, he will be among friends. Actually, observing her impromptu visits to the Floodhouse and the pottery, I am increasingly unsure whether this word can contain the feelings Julie harbours for my father. But that's another story; one my father isn't telling.

By the following afternoon, the rising river water has abated sufficiently to return to the Floodhouse. Back up the willow-strewn valley road we go in my father's Beetle. The river gods haven't laid claim so much as lapped at the lino, spooked the rats and possums, forsook the silty fun of making a river-mark four feet up the walls, and retreated. Stripped of personal possessions, the house is a shabby shell.

My father has fashioned a rough clay hand, with a prominent Mount of the Moon running from under the thumb to the wrist. Once fired, he has nailed it, through a hole in the palm, to the raw-timber wall in the hallway. In the palmistry that he occasionally practises on strangers and friends, a plump Mount of the Moon is an indicator of imagination. My father is a palmist and a writer; the clay icon is a subliminal relation of those miniatures medieval people affixed to their doors to designate their trade. It has always spooked me, especially during night passage to the drinking-water buckets in the kitchen.

I look at the clay hand and its nail stigmata now. What was my father thinking? The Floodhouse will not be repossessed.

The talk of recent months resolves into a decision. My father is leaving for Manaroa, where there will be correspondence school and some ad hoc parenting by members of the community for my sister, and the possibility of an *intense relationship* for him. His words. We have steeped in talk of Manaroa, and the Manaroans, for so long that the remote community has become everything that Canvastown is not. Around our core certainty of the commune's reparative qualities drifts a cumulus cloud of not-quite-fully-formed hopes: the atmospheric expectation of romance and organic vegetables, guitar music and conversation, conducted within an egalitarian and mostly money-free economy. In my family's talk of Manaroa, we are future-dosing ourselves against loneliness and poverty.

But now I put my foot down. Correspondence school supervised by the Manaroans? That sounds *loose*. I decide on the spot that I won't be going to Manaroa, but to Nelson to put myself through the final year of school. University has long been in my sights. Despite the lost ground that is 5A, my appetite for learning remains undiminished. This takes precedence over the Manaroans. Despite their magnetic attraction, there is no contest.

PART 2
Nelson

The Thin Shop

As sometimes happens, my father and I are mistaken for brother and sister. We are on the road and this misrecognition, which makes me older than my years, is intoxicating. What we both register as flattering also conceals a half-truth. In many ways my father, with his open, unlined face, *is* tellingly like an older adolescent brother. One absorbed in his own semi-dormant secret life.

We are hitchhiking to Nelson to check the Thin Shop noticeboard for a room for the school year. There, we meet Robert, a twenty-one-year-old macrobiotic serving behind the counter, who happens to have a spare room to rent in his flat. With black corkscrews falling across his face, Bugs Bunny front teeth and a sudden, solipsistic laugh, Robert is goofily attractive. The interview takes place on the health-food shop floor. Within minutes the encounter has taken on the air of a fait accompli. My father and I arrange to walk across town and look at the room, but this is a formality. Where else am I going to live?

Key decisions in my life often unfold like this. A jump into the unknown with barely a thought as to whether your parachute will open. A pact of shakily tacit confidence on the part of all involved—the role of curiosity not to be underestimated—each thinking that, if the other thinks all is well, *it will be.* My father reassures me this is how you live if you are an artist. On the fly; by your wits. By this credo, at fifteen, I begin my life as an artist, but I would never think to call it that.

A scholarship of two hundred dollars a term, matched by postal cheques from Grandfather Sam, will be just enough to pay my rent and groceries. My grandfather has long approved of my bent for education. Thanks to his beneficence, I will be fiscally empowered, unilaterally in charge of my small, bountiful everything. From their remove, my male relatives have great confidence in me. Enlivened by the prospect of moving in with Robert of the unclipped poodle bangs, the sallying-forth aspect of my nature comes to the fore. Adult life beckons. More—it is about to take me in.

Accompanied by little more than the well-travelled eiderdown and a towel, I move in to Wellington Street a week after the Thin Shop encounter. With two bedrooms, and a sunroom-conversion that is yet to be let, the house is as roomy as a family home and as under-furnished as any student flat. The sparseness doesn't bother me. Not after the Floodhouse's lacks. Without my father as provedore and cook, I reacquaint myself with skills that I learned, thanks to my grandmother's frequent ill health, early in life.

Margaret had high blood pressure, and Martin and I lived in fear of a much-talked-of clot travelling to her heart. For me, this fear was concentrated in the sight of my grandmother's shins. Covered by a thin layer of disturbingly crispy skin, the blood would clot and pool just beneath after the slightest knock. I worried a lot for those shins and, by extension, for my delicate, dramatic grandmother. When she and Martin occasionally scuffled in the hall, it was her shins I feared for. Not that she saw herself as delicate. Outspoken and reliably moved by injustice or social inequity, she was not one to creep around taking self-preserving measures in life.

Once, she came home from a drive around the bays with

Martin to report that she had to pull over to talk down a man threatening to hit his son with a chain out on the rocks at Breaker Bay. *What kind of chain?* I couldn't help asking. I was often curious about details. *A big chain*, she clarified. The man—large, tattooed—had cried, and confided that his father had beaten him as a child. Martin corroborated the encounter in that mostly passive way of his, as if nothing could surprise him. My grandmother hoped she had helped the man see the harm in the cycle of abuse. He was coming over the next week to chat, just in case. She felt he needed further unburdening.

I never met this man, who visited while I was at school, but I was moved by and proud of my grandmother's disarming initiative. It was not the first or last such foray she made. I noticed that these strangers were exclusively men. Men seemed to own the grand emotional narratives in her book. Not men her own age, with whom she was done, but younger men who might need rescuing. Despite her own rich biography as a woman, she didn't especially extend the compliment or concern to her own gender.

I was sensitive to male suffering myself. My father's sighing verbalisations of tiredness, underlined by a reflexive sweep of his hairline with one hand, had affected me since I was small. At four, five, and then six, I knew his complaints were code for something else, for a melancholy that was possibly even more foundational than the rocky state of my parents' marriage. Did *I* make him tired? I worried about my father's all-encompassing tiredness as I later did my grandmother's shins. Martin's increasingly locked-in emotional life was another source of tension. This sense of male suffering, and violence too, crystallised around the image my grandmother brought home that day of the boy and his father out on the rocks.

*

As it turned out, Margaret, her bloodstream's clotting tendencies notwithstanding, lived to ninety-six. In the process, she set me up for life with a cooking habit, and the belief that you could talk to anyone.

Miss Johnson

The first good thing that happens to me at Nelson Girls' College is my new English teacher asks me to read aloud. Reading aloud, the spell of it. I make my voice a soft lure to reel my new classmates in. In fact, it is only Miss Johnson that I hook. Astute, courtly and modest to a fault, Miss Johnson has something of the appeal of a lady writer manqué. Now, her eye alights speculatively on the overthinking new girl who likes to read aloud. This emboldens me.

When Miss Johnson describes the birth of twins as *she produced twins*, I interject. *You make it sound like they came out of a paper bag.* My classmates look at me in consternation. Miss Johnson appears obscurely pleased, but I suddenly feel like a jerk. My English teacher makes me self-conscious, the way she turns the gently mocking eyes of age on my ungently mocking youth.

I think I recognise her perspective now, how it sometimes catches on the possibility of a particular student, the one you think might just out-straddle convention.

This small but accordion-like moment will unfold at sixth-form year's end, and the end, therefore, of my and Miss Johnson's relationship. In the beginning, however, Miss Johnson merely asks me to read texts out loud more and more often.

One afternoon, I have just parsed J. Alfred Prufrock's coffee spoons and passed his love song to the reader in the row behind, when something unexpected happens. Lucy, whose desk is paired with mine, slaps me in the face. In a stinging flush, I see my neighbour's storybook features transformed by hatred. Noses in texts, no one appears to witness the assault. Not even Miss Johnson who, seconds before, directed her small, delphinium-blue eyes at me and said, *You have a lovely voice.*

After that, I stop sitting next to Lucy, whom I had picked out in a dream of tall, interesting-looking girls. For her part, Lucy keeps her chin in the air when I pass. I sense her shame. We share an unwanted secret: the way jealousy charged through Lucy and might do so again. It makes me feel uncomfortably powerful, this knowledge, and Lucy and I stick to ever-widening distances.

Then, only three weeks into term, I catch whooping cough. No more school, no more reading aloud—no more Lucy, either. I am about to do precisely nothing for the next four months.

Perspectives

Whooping cough. I have contracted this novelistic, nineteenth-century illness possibly from my sister during an undetected gestation at the Floodhouse. She is the first to fall sick. After I succumb, my father appears at Wellington Street to take me to meet his friend Christine, who has offered up her spare room. Then he is gone. Not only have we underestimated the scope and scale of whooping cough, but he must return to nurse my sister, a day's travel distant, at Manaroa.

I stay a week or two under the patchwork quilt of Christine's spare room, venturing out to soak up the rays of her bohemian décor, the zinnias in her yard, and her healing regard. Once, we take a picnic to the Maitai River where I socialise with the Nelson Girls' College art and drama teachers, a phenomenon unimaginable at my previous high school. I keep thinking it must look as if I'm playing hooky, but no one bats an eyelid. In this company I am a quasi-adult with volition rather than a lone out-of-school teenager with a Victorian cough.

Thin and burnished with sharp swoops of hair framing her face, percussive bracelets and elongated wrists, always in motion, Christine takes me so deftly under her wing I wish never to leave her house. More, I want to be her. The steep bone tent that pushes up the eaves of her shoulders notwithstanding.

Christine has scoliosis. When she was the age I am now, she was led on to the stage of a university auditorium, where she undressed and submitted to the spectatorship of rows of medical students. Standing there, she was analysed and discussed as an example of her condition. *It was what you did*, she tells me with a painful shrug. *Trusted medical men.* In the silence that follows, I hear her wonder at her extreme vulnerability, and her passivity. I am honoured and touched to find myself the recipient of this harrowing memory—one, she tells me, she has not previously confided. After this, Christine gets on with what needs doing, crossing the darkwood floors of her house in a voluminous smock from another, more painterly era, footsteps quick-stepping in vanishing aural perspective.

My host is a glimpse of the mother I would have liked to have had. Just a glimpse, for soon enough her eleven-year-old daughter, Josie, and her musician husband reassert their rightful place in Christine's affection. It is time for me to move on, back to my room in Thin Shop Robert's flat. I take my cough with me.

Robert samples my hair and nail clippings and wires them into a voodoo healing matrix in two interconnected shoeboxes under my bed. I don't know what to think, but I go along with it anyway, in the spirit of a wacky experiment. It helps that Robert comports himself like a professor.

Days turn to weeks as I lie in my Wellington Street bed. Occasionally, I spare a thought for the bioorganic samplings in open cardboard coffins beneath me, failing to work their magic. Occasionally, my flatmate appears to enquire after any improvement in my health. There is none. Robert's stab in the fantastical dark merely passes time, of which I have a surfeit.

He tinkers with the coffins, warning that overexposure can have the inverse effect and intensify the malady. Not long after this, Robert dismantles the wiring, but leaves the boxes and organic clippings behind. These spurned offerings, which have lost the promise of sorcery along with their circuitry, devolve into undone housework. And that is how they remain, collecting dust but no further discussion.

The shoebox voodoo is one speculative treatment. The homeopath, whom my father finds for me across town, another. Mildly distracted by the allure of the tools of the trade—pendulum and little white pills that dissolve under the tongue—though I am, I cannot imagine these slight means turning back the course of this force of nature: whooping cough. The homeopath's other means of diagnosis—an arsenal of questions—worries me. Am I unusually sensitive to fluctuations of temperature? Morning, evening, or after midnight? Do I crave cold foods, ice cream especially? When? Would I say I was beset by fears? And if so, of the dark, of disasters, or of other people? Permeations of the possible unfurl before me and I become too fancifully taken up with these to answer with any certainty. *Do I? Am I?*

I needn't worry. The cough carries on regardless, whooping in great wheeling revolutions at ever-diminishing intervals. There is more and more time at my disposal, but less and less to breathe. I knock around in the dry dock of my double bed. Going nowhere fast, chasing breath.

The last time I saw Richard

Richard appears at the Wellington Street kitchen table one night, faintly beatific and dressed from head to foot in John Lennon white, right down to his sneakers. This is not merely affectation for Robert and Richard do play tennis together. I spare a thought for what their games might be like: erratic, giggly, surprisingly violent. At our table, however, Richard is softly dazzling, wistful. Later, I will make a friend of the photographer Janet Bayly, who says she realised at sixteen that only egoists wear all white. I am sixteen but I don't yet have Janet's prophylactic insight. I do, however, like to sing along with Joni Mitchell's gorgeously skewering ballad 'The Last Time I saw Richard'.

This Richard is a supple thirty-one, girlishly flyaway hair caught in a tail; a solo dad with an infant daughter he regrets seeing only every other weekend. Somehow, Richard ends up in my bed. It's the only place to visit me after all. Once he is there, I realise Richard is a bore.

After the first visit, I make a line down the bed and don't let him cross it. Amazingly, he abides but keeps showing up on the other side of the line anyway. I can't seem to dislodge

Richard with niceness, my usual weapon. He is passive, persistent, without force. We have a couple of sessions like this. Then I learn blunt. *Please, sorry. Actually, sorry . . . No.* Even I sense I might be looking for a father.

After this, Richard returns to being my flatmate Robert's friend. But direct, staccato, solar-flare Robert is irritated by insinuatingly low status, elliptically recurring Richard, too. Their tennis games end in sulks. Robert, who has a talent for the latter, has met his match in the older man. Soon the two friends are unable to play at all. Then, one day, Richard simply fails to recur.

Return orbit

The countryside unfolds monotonously but the music of transition is mine. I am busing from Nelson to Canvastown across the Whangamoa hills, gloomy with *Pinus radiata*, to convalesce with my sister at the house of former Floodhouse neighbours Bettye and Stu. It will be just me, my father and sister once more, for we are housesitting. In the meantime, sequestered in my travelling cocoon, face pressed to the glass, anything feels possible. I am responsive to the indefinite magic of busing, the suspension of time that, as long as the bus is moving, is its sine qua non.

Stu moved to Canvastown to reinvent himself as a potter. For Bettye, the reinvention was to be motherhood. They arrived a few months after I did from my grandmother's, so for a while I am able to make the most of my superior local experience. Stu is short-levered and brisk; humour set to charge. A practised ruffler of Bettye's settled calm. He and I leave each other alone. Heavy with pregnancy, Bettye is big-featured with large-pored skin, measured movements, and the looks of a Vermeer. She must have fathomed the resemblance, for she dresses in heavy linen and soft cottons in the Dutch painter's palette of French blue, old gold, ochre and cream. Exceptionally, in these sun-worshipping days, she preserves her milky skin under floppy-brimmed hats.

Bettye introduces me to Biba T-shirts and Zandra Rhodes dresses, and other wonders beyond my means or ken. To flowered silk headscarves wrapped tightly about the skull and knotted behind, pirate style. Bettye's hippy chic is urban, moneyed and cites London over the extemporised Eastern European inferences of the Manaroans' gritty style. I can't work her out. She is plain and sovereign, grand and still. Best of all, she invites my schoolgirl orbit. I waste no time in taking up the position.

Occasional afternoons nursing tea-bowls on her velvet sofa offset grotty hours amidst my father's historical grunge. From this vantage, I can run my eyes over the spines of Stu's records, marching upright around the skirting boards of the lounge like a rock 'n' roll army in alphabetical order. Salt-glazed pots by Mirek Smíšek pose as platonic ideals on rimu shelves. After peppermint tea, Bettye sends me to fetch the biodynamic rosehip syrup from the kitchen cupboards, for an immune-boosting chaser. I sprinkle lavender milk from a blue glass Weleda bottle into the claw-foot bath, and Bettye lowers herself heavily in while I keep company on a milking stool.

Sometimes, my father puts on his good shirt and brings my sister to join us. Dressed in her garter-stitch skirt with a yellow crushed-velvet apron, my sister establishes her own watch from the mossy armchair. I can see my father is dismayed by the ceremonial pomp with which Stu unsleeves the bootleg Led Zeppelin or rare Velvet Underground LPs and, not trusting the automatic function, guides the diamond stylus to landing by hand. This is a far cry from my father's suitcase with a needle. Too far. If opulence and display trouble my father, Stu's fastidiousness exhausts him. I watch my father become elusive and exquisitely polite in an effort not to betray his distaste.

It doesn't help that they are both potters. Stu's medium is stoneware, fired at higher temperatures and with less margin for error than the earthenware my father turns on his wheel. Pottery magazines and art catalogues, scattered strategically about, attest to Stu's drive to be numbered among the international pottery cognoscenti. My father, who knocks out his bowls and mugs with good-enough dexterity, shows only sporadic interest in art pottery, and impatience at all shows of expertise. For each man, the other misses the point.

In Stu and Bettye's world of showcased objects, my father is a pip of unease, a wild seed disseminating untidiness. But I give him this—he carries his elegance below the radar. You only need to see him on the dance floor to know that. His classic rock 'n' roll moves are light, scrupulously attentive and indelibly sunny. I wish I could dance like that.

With our hosts absent, my father, convalescing sister and I unconsciously remake Bettye and Stu's household in our shambolic image. I spend hours down among Stu's LPs, mucking with the indexing system while swotting cover art and band pics, lowering discs imprecisely onto prestige turntable. Sometimes I rifle through Bettye's wardrobe, getting high on texture and pattern, the sense of trespass so intense that eventually the room hums and I have to leave.

Mostly I can be found drifting in the spare room's cast iron bedstead. Sometimes I muse on the gap between the order of the décor and Bettye's confidences, which swirl like patches of white-water around fears for her marriage. The latter centre on an ex of Stu's, a prostitute of unmatched sexual powers, or on the short financial leash on which Stu's society-matron mother keeps her son. The power of these other women over pugnacious Stu gives Bettye, and by association me, pause. That other power, of scintillating cliché, goes unremarked.

Occasionally my father appears with beetroot salad and omelette, or to pour precious rosehip syrup down my throat in service of the whooping cough that won't release me from its revolutions. Alone again I wank. I am doing this when Bettye pops her head around the door.

We're back!

Early.

Bettye's eyeline travels straight to the spot under the heavy white damask spread where my hand plays dead.

Not long after Bettye's exit, my father appears, harassed. We're off sooner than he had imagined. The drastically reduced levels of rosehip syrup, the violated LP indexing, the velvet sofa cushion sporting plate with browning pear core, the kitchen floor rich in recent crumbs, have not impressed our returning hosts.

The mirror

While we are at Bettye and Stu's, my mother visits with Heinz. My father carries Bettye's wicker chairs out to the paddock behind the house, knowing my mother has a liking for these knitted pieces of Victoriana. In the early days of their marriage, my mother and he shared an eye. Maybe it even kept them together: that and their summary judgements of others. They would pick up Bentwood chairs, and other pieces not yet classed as antiques, from the side of the road. Some found their way to our house; others they sold. Once, they found forty dollars, a tidy sum in 1968, sewn into the hem of a pair of junk-shop velvet curtains.

It is from one of these wicker thrones that my artfully arranged mother gives audience. If she is nervous, I have no sense of it, but I haven't yet learned to read her inner signs. Nor she mine. It will take decades of further separation before we are able to decode that subtle language. In the field behind Bettye and Stu's, only my mother's fierce outer signs reach me. In turn, I cultivate round shoulders on the grass. A faint hope lurks beneath my physical defences. Has my mother come because of the Cough?

Actually, my mother has got wind of my relationship with a man old enough to be my father. I wish I could reassure her that unworldly Richard is almost more of girl than I, and one I have disposed of, besides, but I am a surly configuration of mute adolescent particles.

What disturbs my mother is that I am having sex. I am *too young for sex.* It has clearly made me ill, *for that is what sex without love does.* I am *a child who needs her bottom smacking and sending home.* I suck in my mother's words and spit the salient one out. *Home?* Home is a vexed category. She has no right to use such a term in relation to me.

The dissonance of my mother's words is compounded by the erotic style of her dress. How can this outré sex symbol be so discomfited by my unhappy fumbling with Richard? Besides, Richard came *after* the Cough. And, even though the sex—all sex—thus far has been crap, I recoil from so punitive a view. I'm sticking out for future good times. I'm defending my own small corner of fuck-ups.

I know little of the particulars of my mother's falling out

with her mother over her own teenage sexuality, or the way her certainty that I am repeating her own high dive into adult business worries the blade of her words razor-sharp. I am just the age she was then. All I hear is her judgement. My mother's face is tilted my way, but it is impossible to meet her rapidly blinking eyes. Her buffered, rebuffing gaze has been this way since I can remember.

As a small child, I was hungry to intercept that gaze. I would position myself a few feet off to the side when my mother stood before the mirror to dress. From this lateral position I would stare directly upwards into the glass, hoping to insert myself in the loop of her self-regard. This was no game for either of us. It was long duration, my mother's assessment, and it didn't include me. Made doubly self-conscious by my presence, her blinking would quicken as she surveyed facets of herself with queenly displeasure. If I was stuck there, she was too. Time froze and flickered in the glass. Day after day we would repeat our silent witnessing, our deferral of intimacy, our lonely battle of the eyeline.

Now, in the face of my mother's angry connection of sex, sickness and home, I look away across the thistle paddock. My mother and I are two vectors arrowing sharply off. It will be years before we see each other again.

Strawberry blonde

A very tall strawberry blonde with a beauty spot, as spitefully angular as an Aubrey Beardsley drawing, has asked me out on a date. Tom is my own age. It's like a job interview for Normal. I pose in front of my wardrobe mirror in a brown felt hat the shape of an inverted flowerpot. Tiny flowers spill over the rayon housecoat that I wear unbuttoned over trousers. I'm going for urban hippy chic with a flash-forward to Diane Keaton's Annie Hall. Not a look I am experienced in. Buoyed by my participation in an archetypical adolescent activity, I am prepared to bluff it out.

Outside the Hitching Post café, one of Nelson's few places to see and be seen at night, Tom makes a sulky scan of my get-up. It seems to make him angry, but I convince myself this is simply first date nerves. Mine and maybe even his. Once inside, I truck optimistically on, ebullient and conversationally unaccompanied, compounding my sartorial glitch by talking about my parents. It is not cool to talk of parents as if they are cool. It is a mirage, this parental coolness, one that only shimmers in absence, but Tom doesn't know this.

Or maybe he does, and decides I am a phony. Perhaps he is even more judgemental than I. Either way, Tom does not reply to my enquiries into his life or family. I have the feeling of colliding with an especially solid piece of code, one I have not had the opportunity to decipher. Conversation flickers, gutters and extinguishes as prematurely as the utility-white candle thrust in a bottle at our table.

I don't get the position for Tom's girlfriend. For Normal. On reflection, nor do I want it. I return to Wellington Street early, vowing never to wear that ridiculous, old-lady hat again.

At the river

One empty afternoon, towards the end of convalescence, I accept an invitation to the Maitai River from a smiling, hippy drop-in to Wellington Street. He must have come looking for Robert, but to insist on compartmentalising acquaintance is not the done thing. The muddy shallows of the Maitai are on the scrappy side, but the visitor has wheels, and I nowhere else to be.

On the cold river stones, the visitor strips off and sits displaying his erection with the look of an ill-favoured minor deity who has produced a miracle. Embarrassed not to have understood the point of the journey, I inexpertly oblige. The hand job is desultory, and over very fast. Men don't seem to notice or care that you don't desire or even especially like them.

Business done, the tatty-haired one drives me home. I roll the passenger seat window right down. Now that the dynamics of the encounter have been laid bare and, at least to his mind, resolved, we do not speak.

The breeze is my friend: motiveless, caressing, travelling on. I lean into it, hoping to get there soon.

School interludes

Dick Nunns, pony-tailed drama teacher, says I have the laugh of a forty-year-old woman. I am drinking cold grape juice at Chez Eelco with the other drama students and fielding an ice-cream headache. As soon as he says this, I fall off my barstool.

In D. Nunns's improvisation class, I choose older men to act out, characters who are sleazy but ineffectual, and whom I am surprised to become. They leave an uneasy residue. Not least from my own overacting.

A former minister, recently self-declared pacifist and vegetarian, the history teacher shares the teaching of our class with an ascetic Rhodes Scholar. They are each inspiring, these co-teachers, in their different ways. The Rhodes Scholar is brilliant and personally unassailable. The pacifist is impulsive, coquettish, and throws a duster at me in class when I overstep the mark with teenage irony. Blushes and hurls. My relationship with authority is ambivalent, but the pacifist makes us feel he is one of us. His expertise turns swiftly to doubt and, just as suddenly, gaiety. I like him even more once I know he has poor impulse control.

When the year is done I am awarded First Prize in History and First Equal in Art. Changes of address, a term's absence, and my experimental sexuality have not wreaked the expected havoc with my concentration. I have been cultivating the latter since I was a small child at school and my parents were home unpicking each other. When I wasn't worrying at personal facts—my parents' personal facts—I was busy reading, writing and doing the drawings my mother liked to see me do. Turning whatever pages were at hand, covering others with cursive or biro portraits of family members in elaborate frocks, time opened into a bloom and took me inside.

At Nelson Girls' I am befriended by Tracey, who has visions of the future she wishes she didn't. Troubling visions concerning other people's troubles, after which she doesn't sleep. She is surprisingly neat and practical-looking for a psychic, Tracey, and is taking accounting. Only her uncanny eyes give her away. She comes to find me in the school grounds each time she has a vision, because, she says, I am the only one who believes her. And I do. She and I are not friends in any usual sense. Instead, our lives have this single intersecting node. Huddled on the asphalt playground, we incline our heads, witches in school uniform, before going our separate ways.

Thanks to whooping cough I have a single term to complete the entire sixth-form curriculum. Of greater concern is money.

Along with school assignments I bring home sheafs of vintage garments with which to supplement my breadline scholarship by darning signs of wear, hand-stitching hems and anchoring stray sequins for a retro clothing shop. I have always been economically resourceful, and now I am taking in sewing: a fleeting instalment in my twentieth-century identification with nineteenth-century heroines. It is probably illness that first triggers this sympathy. When I read *The House of Mirth*, I feel the complex portrait of laudanum and female tragedy—temperamental, social, economic, class-bound—so keenly, Lily Bart threatens my imagined future prospects. Once imbibed, laudanum does not leave your system but accrues until the fatal dose is unwittingly reached. There is a metaphor here and I feel sure it applies to me.

I have had a special interest in poisons since childhood when I worried I would sleepwalk and swallow the bottle marked *Not To Be Taken* in the bathroom cupboard.

For my own mental health, I go no further with Edith Wharton.

My work for the vintage clothes shop stands me in good stead for the Nelson Girls' graduating formal. Dressed in a black pin-tuck muslin tent dress, pink sequin bolero and strappy stilettos on loan from the proprietor, I am a proud child of the seventies. My friend from drama, Ruth Belton, has arranged a date for me through her Nelson Boys' contacts—I have none of my own. Mark is a sulkily pretty boy with snarled eyelashes of whom it is impossible to know much because he never speaks. In the risible way of teen sexual hierarchies, he is considered a catch. I think Mark beyond my reach, but Ruth makes the whole arrangement seem easy. A small gang of her friends and I meet on the steps of Nelson Cathedral and hobble the ten minutes to college in a swirl of black and white and impossible shoes. It feels lovely, like something kids in American movies do.

Mark and I have one affectless dance before he crosses the floor to join a blond secretary-type in a leopard-spot cheongsam for the rest of the night. She is older, is not even enrolled at school, but she and my date have previously arranged to meet. I didn't cry on leaving my mother and father, then my grandmother, then my father again. After abandonment on the Nelson Girls' College school hall dancefloor, my tear ducts finally come unstuck.

Busy with their own dates, a small cohort of classmates makes time to close around me. There is always someone by my side. At one point, a blond stranger materialises and offers his arm. A deft mover in a rented tuxedo, he spins me to the far side of the floor and back. I surrender to speed, distant circles and the trope of a handsome stranger. It is enough, this romantic crumb at the feast. After that, I am content to listen to swan-necked Anne van den Berg, wearing actual jewels, describe the five men she is currently dating, each unbeknownst to others. This trance-like girl forgoes dancing to train her lashed-wide gaze on mine. Escaped from the Social Pages, Anne is unusually tall, poised. She is either a liar or a sociopath, or just very good at dating.

Weeks on, I visit the downtown photographer who holds a card file of contact prints from the night. There I am imprisoned in a small grey rectangle in the narrow cardboard box, smiley in sequins. I think I look too young for my age. Do I mean overly trusting? That too.

And there he is, cynically in possession of his other objectives. I feel chagrined for subscribing to a valuation—his—that I never believed in. I refrain from purchasing the reminder.

The art teacher's wife

In Art as in life, I am obsessed with birds. For a while I was going to be an ornithologist. Zoologist then ornithologist come after Egyptologist in the deck of childhood aspirations.

In Pete Belton's big-windowed art room where I am free to come and go, I scratch inky Rotring drawings, treetops squalling with blackbirds. This is the privilege of my last and only term at Nelson Girls': trusted to work alone. I dig out the linocut grooves of a sleeping woman curled on her side, a crow standing watch on her haunch. Deb, an adult student with orange hair and lost eyes, poses for the figure. *Birds are signs of the soul*, advises Pete, referencing Van Gogh. I become more obsessed with birds.

I visit Deb, who rents a shepherd's hut on a painter's farm on the outskirts of Nelson. The painter is a streak of glamour sighted from across the fields. A landed pixie. I observe Deb from closer up, her suede skirts and posh sentences that sometimes falter. We go to a club in downtown Nelson where my greatest fear is that Deb will give me an unsolicited shoulder massage while we are sitting on bean bags listening to the music. In the event she embarks on a head massage and ruins my hair instead.

Sometimes I go around to the art teacher's house for Sunday lunch or afternoon tea. His is a double-fronted Victorian whose entrance hallway is long enough to play cricket on, but for a film-set flurry of hat stand, coat rack and other explosions of bourgeois mess. It is here that you become aware you are entering a *household*. Even without the wisteria wafting aromatic spore from the back terrace, this simple fact is narcotic.

Pete Belton's wife is a children's illustrator. With a bouffant that adds quarter her diminutive height again,

Cleopatra eyeliner, an amount of facial powder that quotes the Elizabethans, and a waist fiercely accented by belted full skirts and overhanging stalactites of lace, Robyn Belton is an illustration herself. That the bouffant appears slept in only adds value. Speaking rapidly in whispery sentences, she moves as fast as her line. Inviting me into her study at the bottom of the hall, she offers a glimpse of a work-in-progress for School Journals. A careening circle of figures engage in slapstick chase, overturning flowerpots, smashing crockery as they liberate themselves from their author's reflexive uncertainty. I take note of her freehand line. Coloured by strategically approximate blobs of watercolour—crimson jacket here, pair of black Dickensian boots churning air there—the completed artwork retains the insouciance of a sketch.

After lunch, we watch an antique spinning top painted in chipped circus colours, the size and circumference of a child's head, hum as it builds speed. Robyn has purchased the tin top as research for an illustration and, as side-effect, an amusement for her young son. Now she hovers, hands on hips, sleeves turned up, like a mater from times past mesmerised by the spell of centrifugal force.

After repeat exposure, I conclude that, for all their whirring sound and motion, husband and wife are as shy as me. Their sentences trail off into the tacit. Robyn's, feathery and self-extinguishing. Pete's, bolstered with subclauses, qualifiers and other self-interrupting quests and struts of deprecating erudition. Do I want to be part of this household? Only for the brief time I am in it. My fantasies function like camouflage, taking on the protective colouring of whichever environment they fetch up in.

Inheritances

I pack the Chinese red, floor-length damask tent-dress for drama camp. The dress has come to me by way of Maddy, on whose family cherry orchard in the Māpua hills, west of Nelson, I have recently been a weekend guest.

How could I know that my grandfather Patrick Hayman, of whose existence I am yet unaware, visited and bicycled in these same Māpua hills as a brown-limbed young man with Colin McCahon and friends in the late 1930s? Such tracks make the New Zealand landscape a palimpsest, if only you knew where to look for them.

I meet Maddy in D. Nunns's drama class, where I am magnetised by her casually radiant expectations. It helps that my classmate is made from seamless, honey-coloured stuff. Mellifluous stuff. Habitually bare feet. Boys follow her around but fail to get under that bright skin. At the time of my Māpua visit, there are two contending: the boy with snarled eyelashes with whom I will attend my formal and who Maddy is, even now, pre-emptively deflecting my way; and her actual boyfriend, a political science student who she is about to give the flick. In relation to these boys and their object, I am a mirror that, tilted the right way, might afford a flash of the sun.

Back on our own again, we loll in the bunks of one of the seasonally vacant cherry pickers' cabins and are visited by her Swedish, clog-wearing mother and soigné friends. This trio of women has dropped by for a viewing and become implausibly interested in my complexion. I think they must have rocks for brains. Who cares about skin?

Of greater, prurient interest to me and my new friend are the scarlet walls of the parental bedroom, hung with soft-centre paintings. Otherwise empty but for the sprawling bed, the room has been staged and colour themed by Maddy's mother. The sexuality of parents is monstrous, but Maddy and I pretend to be the cool libertarian teenagers we are not. The red is the thing, a statement of sexiness unlike anything I have encountered. It makes the hippy milieu look dour; nature adulation has a puritanical streak. Torn as I am between cynic and voluptuary, the scarlet signifier hovers in my speculation all weekend long. You have to be Swedish, I conclude, to be so unabashed in allure, so undemure in cliché.

I return to Wellington Street with the loan of Maddy's dress, in whose borrowed folds I have spent the weekend. After that, I see Maddy less and less. Impressions linger of the family estate, with its cool-blooded social configurations, financial expectations and cruelly dashing sexual mores. One visit and I have gleaned how embedded in a world beyond my compass and means Maddy actually is. I am beginning to understand enough about social form not to press for friendship, despite her overtures, for this is precisely all they are—gestures without intent. And yet, Maddy understands the debt of gratitude. She is as keen to extend the complex sign of the red dress as I am to accept it.

About the same time that I am packing the glowing tent, Ruth Belton, my art teacher's younger sister, is packing her late mother's wedding dress. This is a snake of pale blue, peach-flowered silk georgette with an excess of tiny covered buttons running down the back, the gored skirt trouncing ankles.

A doctor's daughter on both sides, Ruth Belton lives in a mansion whose second-storey balcony is wound so densely in flowering vines one can disappear behind their tangle. And that's what we do whenever I walk over on the weekend: sit behind the fall of foliage and conspire. She has kinky lips and dark, springy hair. We are sixteen and seventeen. Neither of us has a boyfriend. Ruth calls me *Brainbox* and *Mouse*, and we share unspoken versions of the motherless wound. Ruth's mother died when she was young, and in the case of her benign, professionally distracted stepmother, it is a lesser intimacy.

Now I will be returning to my hometown for drama camp and doing so in uneasy anonymity, for I will not visit my grandmother there. The silence between me and Margaret has hardened into something unbreakable—and fragile, too. I say nothing of this to anyone, but the storm cloud in my chest is eased by Ruth, who is going with me.

At Downstage Theatre, the first night of camp, I watch men watch Ruth as we take our seats. Her mother's wedding dress is sheer, Ruth's breasts and bikini elastic defiantly on show. Ruth, herself, is elastic, I think, as I watch the way she moves, never alights, never makes herself quite available but participates generously in all. When we get back to the school hall where we are dossing down on the bare floor in our sleeping bags, Ruth shimmies out of her dead mother's wedding dress and gives it to me. Just like that.

Too far out

I look down on my shouty, melodramatic self. I am on stage and have just discovered that the complex present with its recent-past maternal line rejections doesn't lend itself to third-rate student actors, staging and direction, let alone entertainment. I have confused trauma for drama. In the thick of semi-autobiographical improvisation, I am suddenly outside myself. Unsure of how to get back except by compounding the exposure, I keep going.

It is my experience that if you swim out too far in this world—a late-seventies, anything-goes world—no one comments, certainly not the adults. The zeitgeist is in favour of letting it out, letting it happen, letting it roll. In the absence of popular wisdom regarding what happens next, you tread water and cope with the fallout. This is how it is for us kids. We let the dramaturgy unravel. Then we climb offstage, where I slip unobserved into a turbation of shame.

At the film and acting school where I teach as an adult, I recently heard a counsellor describe a variety of student who enrols with hopes of becoming an actor, but in whom the acting process reveals a damaged core. The latter, she explains, manifests in the involuntary crossing of boundaries during performance.

What are the signs to look out for? an acting teacher wonders.

The counsellor, who is statuesque and robustly gestural, sits uncharacteristically still, arms pinned to her side, head hung by way of demonstration. *Deep shame after self-exposure. Head hung as the student descends into self-hate*, she glosses. Secure in my teacher's chair in the training-day circle, the counsellor's words hark back to my young actor self on the Karori School Hall stage, the raw material of life and self dangerously in play. *Weeping continuously, even during another's performance*, the counsellor finishes her list. That wasn't me. Mine was the silent, internal drop.

The counsellor holds the room with her physical articulations. I recognise, in her account of shame, my own. I have it still, am still unprepared for the flash flood that can wake me in the night. Shame is a burden and, sometimes, a source of things to be investigated further in creative work. It is a homeopathic principle to inoculate yourself with a controlled amount of the pathogen you wish to outstep, but, at sixteen, I haven't the faintest idea how to calibrate either the dose or the boundaries between life and art.

Sitting in the teacher circle, I recognise the counsellor's imagery but reject the way the matter trips off her tongue. *Damaged core* connotes the irretrievable. It would not have helped me to be diagnosed this way at sixteen, nor does it help to think it now. You learn to live with assaulting vulnerability. To let its snowstorm snow you, its fear frighten you, its Diablo bedevil you, and pass on.

After our improvisation, a student from Auckland, Miles—angular and proto-punk—does absurdist imitations of his army dad. The routine is funny. We all relax. I lose myself, happily, in contemplation of Miles and his talent. I don't realise it yet, but this tall, mercurial boy is my type. Amidst the ocean of sleeping bags, Miles and I discover how to zip ours together. We fool inexpertly around, and then Miles snakes down the quilted cocoon and goes down on me. My previous sexual encounters have been fleeting, one-sided, unsustained. This is intimate. Cunnilingus is intimate. But no sooner is the intimacy over than a wave of nausea swamps me. How completely unknown to me is Miles, and I to him.

A matter of weeks later, Miles flies from the top of one island to the top of the other to visit me in my town. I have sex with him that afternoon. It is more a failure of imagination than anything else. Miles is anarchic, vulnerable and has hyper theories about everything. I like this only, lonely child of a military father, but we are strangers in a rush to be otherwise.

After sex in my daytime bed, I feel an animal panic. I have no idea how to overcome the overexposure or the anxious desire to please Miles. All I can think of is to catch the bus alone to Tahunanui Beach.

Windy, deserted, and inhospitable mid-week, the white sand stretches. Curled around myself like one of the koru I coveted in the Waiheke hills as a child, I lie listening to the roaring void I am. Eventually, I tune in to the unempathic, rhythmically assertive sound of the big breakers. Eventually, the sheer elemental force of the place restores me.

Spectrum

I am in my forties by the time my friend Doris McIlwain tells me there is a known spectrum for sensory and psychological porousness. I have just confided my tendency to disappear into others, to blot up atmospheres and emotions. Doris offers that I must be way down the receptive end of the spectrum, where she is too. We are on the phone at the time. I, rounding the darkening sports oval at the bottom of my street; Doris, driving across the city. I am elated that such a thing is *known.*

I still have trouble with boundaries. Maintaining, observing and distinguishing them. Now Doris has given me a scale. Not only does such a spectrum exist but it sports degrees and a name. Briefly the miasma of overidentification, of permeability, is subject to the mirage of order. What a relief. I am so impressed by Doris—academic, psychotherapist and amateur potter—and her apposite well of arcane information that I fail to memorise the name of the spectrum.

Now, like Doris, who died very suddenly of a rare kidney cancer, the name of the spectrum has deserted me. It is only a pinprick of loss, the name, compared to and magnified by the loss of Doris herself, but I am shocked by the unaccounted-for information that goes with her. Words *do* die with people.

What this means for me is that in resuming namelessness, the tendency to disappear into some *other* thing or person resumes its ontological lack of borders.

Older women

From first appearance at Wellington Street Lisa makes a strong sensory impression. Almond and rose oils rise off her skin, generating a bouquet reminiscent of my mother's. This predisposes me towards Thin Shop Robert's on-and-off-again girlfriend—that and her terse Glaswegian wit.

Robert's affair with Lisa incandesces out of nowhere, then peters out once she takes the measure of his emotional capacity. She continues to playfully tolerate my flatmate anyway: his Bugs smile and dark hirsute, his Uranian enthusiasms. I'm glad because this means Lisa still occasionally sleeps over. Then, suspending her salty deadpan, she casts a friendly eye on my stuck-in-between, my girlhood.

For my sixteenth birthday she gives me Cabochard in a curvaceous phial collared by glass bow. Having never possessed such a thing, I instantly spill half of it and mop it up with a handful of dresses. It's a good save. The musk of Cabochard and, by association, Lisa, infuses the rest of the year. It is the year of *Dire Straits: The Studio Album*. Lisa and I go to dances held in the town hall, at the bottom of Nelson's main street, where the band plays 'Down to the Waterline' and 'Southbound Again'. Mark Knopfler's phrasing is a relative of Dylan's, and the band does Bob too: 'One More Cup of Coffee' and 'Mozambique' from *Desire*. My father would approve. There's even a stand-in for Scarlet Rivera's soaring violin.

I could dance all night; although, you don't dance with Lisa so much as circulate on the periphery of her narrow-hipped, wide-stanced, don't-fuck-with-me solo. I don't think Nelson knows what to do with this level of feline self-possession. Assertive-bodied, graceful, given to sudden rapid fronts of emotional weather, Lisa. How do you get to *be* her?

It is Lisa who has the temerity to crack that other ineffable solitary, Eddie Fox. Eddie's is a significant presence at the Nile Street dances. Tantalisingly in check; his sudden, byzantine courtesies; the Welshman to her Scot. How could Lisa fail to notice him? The two most brilliant-looking people in Nelson—the combination appeals to my masochistic adolescent logic. And yet the thing is shrouded in unfathomables. Perhaps that's what draws them together then drives them apart—that and Eddie's reflexive state of siege. Whatever the cause, Lisa has another of her losses of patience concerning the romantic viability of Eddie Fox.

Despite her quick-draw irritability, I take note of Lisa's evident tenderness for her ex-lovers. In my world, relationships end suddenly with a severe dashing of reputation, usually mine, and without comeback. Despite her evident volatility, I invest Lisa with the hope of longevity. That is, I hope to retain her.

After all, I am the repository of Lisa's confidences: the connection of her digestion to her emotions; the excessive period pains that wrack her pelvis and send her, cyclically, to bed; her tense vulnerabilities and food sensitivities; her fluctuating confidence and energy; the relation of celibacy, solitude and sexual expression to the healing process and her journey (her words). Lisa's solipsism is scintillating. Less so, the Louise Hay affirmations she has recently taken up. I cannot believe that simply because you might repeat, *Every day, in every way, I am becoming* (insert wish fulfilment here), it will be so. If Lisa's therapeutic self-absorption stops short of turning me off, this is because she reliably kicks me out of her room. Even when I have walked over to her Nile Street flat expressly to visit her. She likes to bathe in solitude.

Carpet swoon

I like switching on the radio to hear the official tones of new flatmate Julie recounting a national disaster, or maybe just the local weather, and thinking, *I flat with that voice.* At twenty-one, Newsreader Julie is a rare emissary from the professional world, visiting our lunar-calendar-swotting Wellington Street fringe.

One afternoon after school, I tumble around on the living-room carpet with Thin Shop Robert. From what I have observed, Robert has a prolific but staccato sexual life: effervescent, numerically agile, short duration. Julie joins us in the carpet tumble. She is abstract, Newsreader Julie, with a way of swimming into focus on you and then, less flatteringly, swimming out again. Robert, she and I engage in a three-way heavy pet in the furniture-challenged living room. It is my first experience of sustained foreplay—of any foreplay at all—and I like it. It is a young animal romp; sadly, never to be repeated with these players. This is a paradox that resists my unravelling, the one-time thing whose desirability is intensified because no more is forthcoming.

As serial blond northern travellers stumble in broken English through his bed, Ruth Belton and I exchange intelligence on Robert. He practises an effective opener to seduction with tarot cards, alternative medicine and foot massage. *Tacky shtick*, agree Ruth and I, honing our cynicism on the whetstone of Robert. But even we can see that the bangs help his cause. He's like a standard poodle bounding in the park. Bouncy, sniffy, ears flapping—indifferent.

When I join Julie resting in bed before her evening Radio Nelson shift, the talk turns to our bodies. Recently, a man called Bill has compared Julie's body to that of a lioness. Bill is a bone of contention between Julie and her lawyer-friend, Jeanette, who has a quick-thinking professional reserve and the kind of wiry intent that hooks clients and lovers fast. They either vie over the lovers or share them, Julie and Jeanette. Privately, I conclude Julie is more passionately engaged by her friend than all the lovers combined.

Julie yawns in her Wellington Street sunroom bed, lioness indeed, with pleasure in self. To my mercenary eye, the one that women routinely turn on themselves and each other, Julie lacks a waist and has undefined arms, but these flaws melt before confidence, its transformative tricks of the light. Can I trade my excoriating critical for some of this? I lie still, in a cloud of wondering, until Julie rolls over and terminates our golden hour. Time to pad off and dispense another shot of news.

Jewels

I am eating oranges and yoghurt only this month, whatever the meal. Dogged by indigestion, I have fallen in with a naturopath whose dietary exclusions see me weeding evermore variety from my diet. Admittedly, the extremity of the interpretation is my own. Once again, *white death* is part of my lexicon. With this throwback to early childhood and my parents' conviction that all processed foods are carcinogenic, I am back on the path of dietary zealotry, a route that is reassuringly familiar—less so the square-looking American 'doctor' in nylon clinic coat. Is he a quack? He prescribes drops of hydrochloric acid and grapefruit in the morning to aid my stomach's acid–alkaline balance. For a while these seem to help. Engaged in my doublethink, failing to quite suspend disbelief, I persist in several visits to the naturopath's rooms.

In the middle of my sabbatical from most foods, Jewels visits. The daughter of Manaroan Sylvie, Jewels takes white toast with Vegemite and instant coffee for breakfast. The less wholefood the better. She has surprisingly suburban tastes for a hippy icon. Nor does she do school. The first time I met her was a year or so previous when she visited the Floodhouse, her party-animal father's aloof, sylvan shadow. Her parents had been separated for some time by then, and Jewels was living at Tahuna commune with her father. Despite this correspondence, and the fact that we are the same age, we couldn't be more unalike. For one thing I am still, visibly, a child.

Jewels appears to have shed the evidence of childhood early. Her father, Ken, has a cultured English accent, hedonistic appetites, and the kind of masculine glamour that belongs to cinema. These give him a fair amount of sway—we are not as post-colonial as we like to think—but not with that teetotalling sceptic, my father. Jewels is something else. Steelier, less affected than her dad by the push–pull of others' opinions. In an early show of independence, young Jules changed the spelling of her name, and Jewels she has been ever since.

She turns up at Wellington Street in a stream of bias-cut emerald silk velvet, bearing a dimpled bottle of Leed Lemonade and a disaffected air. My conversational attempts mostly end in a shrug from Jewels. With an affectless way at odds with her naiad looks, she doesn't share my drive to analyse. Perhaps

Jewels and I would like to trade stories, but we don't. At this point the stories are telling us. So we hang out instead, an art Jewels is supreme in. It is impossible not to marvel at her cool loveliness. Quite a bit of time passes in this way before she accepts my invitation to sleep the night in Julie's empty bed. It is as if an Abyssinian cat has decided to stay over.

In the morning, Jewels is unfussed about the absence of coffee and toast on offer in Wellington Street's kitchen. Ours is a little like a one-night stand to which breakfast is an irrelevance. Off into the empty, early-morning Nelson light Jewels lopes, while I get ready for school. I sense I won't see her again. This makes her memorable: the rarity of sightings, the mysterious mundanity of the exchanges.

Much later, I hear that she gets herself back to school, several schools, and becomes a lawyer. Despite the name, Jewels was never going to become a casualty of hippy formlessness.

Coming and going

In this culture of comings and goings, the sheer number of people I become acquainted with is wildly inverse to the number I retain. This perpetual gaining and shedding leaves a powerful imprint. I am situationally agile, far more so than when I left my grandmother's. My observational eye has been piqued. There is anxiety, too.

From childhood friends the severance is so abrupt that it is as if an invisible soundproof curtain falls between myself and that part of my life. The wonder is that I don't try to peer around this barrier more. The radical present claims my attention instead. When the time comes to leave Canvastown, however, I am blue. I realise that the raft of civilisation that is my friendship with John Hadwen will break up once I shift to Nelson. Even more than the steep barrier of the Whangamoa hills, my new life will come between us.

Actually, he and Sue do visit Wellington Street with their toddler Ben, not long after I arrive. We drive to Tahunanui where there is a children's playground in the sand dunes, and where John satirises the awkward set of expectations that attach to the visit. Caught between the roles of father, husband and high-jinks friend, he manages to make us laugh, but otherwise—the playground furniture sinking up to its knees in the dunes, John monkeying about on the monkey bars, the tidy way we shake the sand out of our shoes and climb prematurely back into the van—everything is sad about this visit.

It will be many years before I accept that our friendship had its time and place. By then John Hadwen will have been subsumed by another child and then another marriage, a move to America and back again, an art career, and an early death by cancer in his fifties. Some of this I read about, almost none of it do I witness firsthand. After our trip to the beach I see him three more times, always in a crowd. By that stage I am a woman in my late twenties, and John treats me with a diffidence that is irreconcilable with any past or future intimacy. He was right in predicting my life would get better. I just didn't realise it would be without him.

Last days of Wellington Street

Julie shifts into Lisa's flat, a fifteen-minute walk away on the other side of Nelson Cathedral and in the neighbourhood of my school friend Ruth. Robert melts away. The owners of

Wellington Street, Jean and her husband, are moving back in and have invited me to stay on for the remainder of the school term. There'll be no more hippy travellers—no more random men with girlish hair, professing brotherhood but actually seeking a hand job—hiking up the drive.

Literally overnight I become a guest in a high-functioning household where, formerly, I was among slovenly equals. I have become accustomed to being chief shopper, cook and bottle washer, my flatmates' talents stopping wilfully short of the domestic, my school-goer playing responsible to their extended post-adolescence. I don't begrudge this. Robert and Julie brought home the Information. Now I am redundant. Jean does everything: cooks, cleans and shops while maintaining a take-no-prisoners intelligence *and* the baby.

My father takes immediately to Jean when he visits. She is just the kind of woman he admires: abrasive, intelligent, burdensomely capable. English. They talk at the kitchen table for what seems like hours: books and, this being my father, *relationships.* In the glow of the other's attention, each is an accomplished flirt. It is vaguely disturbing, and I leave them to it. There's not a skerrick of self-mythologising at work with Jean or her husband, and no Information to be gleaned either.

Jean has, from a previous marriage, two teenage daughters and a son, who live out of town with their father, Peter. Hazel, Lucy and their brother are famous beauties with improbably rosy cheekbone apples. Sailing home from drama camp I overhear a Cook Strait ferry steward gasp, *Fucking hell, there goes the Madonna*, as Hazel passes. Hazel is in the same year as me at Nelson Girls'. The steward makes a satirical sign of the cross, but not before I see his astonished eyes. The siblings resemble those pretty-coloured cards of Christian saints the worshipful distribute among themselves. I have been known to own a few myself.

When I first arrive in Nelson, their father Peter invites me to stay over on their land, perhaps even to remain. Overlapping circles of acquaintance are generous when it comes to extending hospitality in the hippy community. Jean's ex and their children keep bees, poultry, horses and a huge vegetable garden, and practise a low-key Christianity. Unsure of how to insert myself into their pastoral bliss, I proceed through serial crushes on each of the four. Initially, I settle on father *and* son. I follow one or other of these over the soft green bumps of their land, my head emptying before Theory. Once I recover from the beauty blinding, I realise these men are too drily abstract for my liking.

Hazel is an earthier pedagogue, laboriously captive to notions of how to be good. Her talk circles how things should be versus how they are. It is the rhythm I can't seem to fit: the words that stop and start and plonk on in search of music. Lucy is more garrulous and irreverent, a teen egoist with the habit of laughing at her own jokes. At thirteen, her wit is a loopy riff on her mother Jean's.

Occasionally, one or other of the sisters shares my bed when they visit their mother overnight. We are friendly, Lucy, Hazel and me. I stare involuntarily into the pool of their pooled beauty, but in spite of—or because of—this, friendship never takes. Nothing sticks to them: not intimacy, not me. It is as if their lustre is a physical fact one bounces off and, in my case, dribbles away like a lost ball.

It takes Jean's baby to innocently see me on my way. Accustomed to getting what he wants, Baby James lunges after me while I am engaged in the important business of writing in my diary by the front-room fire. This is the room where Julie,

Robert and I once engaged in our three-way heavy pet. Now it has more furniture.

Now Baby James slaps me flirtatiously in the face. An invitation to play. I slap him lightly back. He roars, offended. Jean is unimpressed. The deal is board and babysitting, and I am not holding up my end.

Next morning, she levels with her characteristic blunt. *You don't seem happy here. Have you got somewhere else you could live?* She has decided to convert my bedroom into a home office for her accountant husband.

Floating again

When my grandmother sent me back to live with my father, four of my Wellington Girls' teachers offered to put me up for the remaining year and a half of high school until University Entrance was complete. If there were time to register these spontaneous acts of hospitality, I might have taken consolation. Instead, I was unsure whether my grandmother's immediate and emphatic *I am not having you live in the same town as me* was a sabotage of these prospects or a source of relief. Imagine living with your teacher—the level of politeness required. No more *You pig!* hurled down the hallway. Crippling. Then my father stepped into the breach, crossing Cook Strait by ferry and recrossing with me in tow.

After Jean's strategic decision to renovate Wellington Street, my father fails to rematerialise. Into this vacuum saunters schoolmate Caroline, a fellow-reader from my form class, to offer me board. I walk over to Caroline's street of pleasant prospects. In free fall once again, I am about to surrender to the mysterious currents and imperatives of fate, chance, and the kindness of near strangers. I am going to meet Caroline's scientist father, administrator mother and sporty brother.

Caroline shows me her room, the room that might become ours. There are single twin beds in matching quilts, china dogs bobbing on a nightstand, and nothing on the pale blue walls. A wave of claustrophobia passes over me. Out in the dining room, Caroline's tweedy mother indicates the dinner table where I will be included each night in their conversational fold, then tactfully disappears. *I'll leave you girls to get on with it.* Only there seems nothing to get on with. Hard as I try, I cannot transport myself to that well-bred table. This is a failure less of vision than of desire.

The bathroom seals the deal. In this immaculate and air-freshened homage to respectability, I am struck by unaccountable nostalgia for my father's long-drop, for the wild squalor of his downwardly mobile dump, where the corners fall to shadowlands and conversation is never less than a strange flower. I do not belong to the intelligent, conventional bourgeois splendour of Caroline's family home. No point arguing with myself; this is a decision made before I even know it. Out on the cottage-garden street, I exhale. I am a warped slip of wilderness, but my own.

Three sisters

Katie's father is a gust of a man who blows through the house—ruffling, refreshing and unsettling its human contents—and is gone. After he and I have established that we will be irrelevant to each other—he travels for work and is often absent—my interview is over, and I am free to move into the Vinke household with its exposed beams, spacious calm and fibre arts. The impulse to do so is as immediate as my failure to take at Caroline's. It helps that Katie, who has inherited her father's powerful physique and air of preoccupation, and I are already friends by proxy. In the year behind me at school, Katie is Ruth Belton's friend.

At the front of the A-frame, a glassed-in sunroom that will be mine grows out of a spring garden of snowdrops. At first, however, Katie's mother Anna suggests I might like to trial her oldest daughter's attic room. Under the eaves, along the winding riverbank road where the bus picks us up early for the eleven-mile trip to school, Katie and I conduct a chafing, squally intimacy that never settles into trust. Submerged rivalry—for Ruth, for primacy—flares with the hormonal cycles that synch now we are roommates. Before long Anna moves me downstairs to the snowdrop room, and I am able to relax back into my own company once more.

I am often sick at weekends and need time alone to daydream, read novels and repair. The end of Whooping Cough has graduated into a non-specific variety of immune system flop that often forces me to bed. Pulled from the slipstream of others and life around me, I nurse a feeling of non-citizenry. Of failure and social shame. I miss out on events, on regular friendship schedules, on follow-through. Later in life, I come across the term *neurasthenic*, a catch-all for physical illness as an expression of unprocessed emotions. Sometimes my body's failure is the only way I *can* process difficult feelings. It is a frustrating business, but something else happens, too, in these temporal drop-outs and lacuna. Tangling in the arms of the flowering quince in the Vinke's outside-in room, this involuntarily solitary is the place inspiration comes.

Sometimes I visit Katie's younger sister in her room. Concerned with the business of making—love-bead jewellery, a submerged jungle gym for the axolotls—she is just emerging from the cocoon of childhood. She has white-blond plaits and water-sign eyes that train receptively on all within their reach. I like swimming around in her swallowed words. Sometimes we three skinny-dip in the river. They enjoy the kind of uninterrupted relation to their own bodies that makes them superb, the sisters. I think to myself that they are the kind of girls who can wear anklets and get away with it.

Sometimes we drop in on the afternoon parties of a collector who lives along the highway in a miasma of broken-down buses, scavenged car parts, dusty tomes and round-the-clock LPs. Beardy, inscrutably older, Dave Mitchell is a nerd who throws parties; an urban hippy, but not a scratch on the Manaroans. The best part about Dave's parties is getting dressed to go. Once there, the sisters and I hang around in Indian skirts and headbands and baffle the uncommitted attentions of a selection of substance-steeped men. We are dismayingly safe among this older crowd. Dave is impeccably uninterested, which is probably why we keep going.

Dark-haired, sensitive as an insect, Katie's mother is the ectomorph centre of the Vinke household, but we don't apply much to her. Like a gentlewoman from another age, she is busy with arts and crafts, reading and reflection and, only occasionally, meals. Alone together, we four women prefer to graze. Sometimes Anna's eye alights on me as if to see what new information I might bring. I do my best to amuse her with bravura pronouncements on the occult or my family, but I am aware of her restlessness. Anna has outgrown motherhood, and maybe the holding pattern of her marriage, too.

In the garden aquarium I dip into an Agee jar of almonds to supplement my vegetarian diet. For the sisters, this private supply is an object of fractious desire, a signifier of independence and share-house flatting histories outside their experience. After some discussion and in mollification of strong feelings aroused, Anna installs another almond jar in the kitchen pantry. I hang on to my personal hoard. It is collateral against the great gifts the sisters enjoy: their beauty and privilege, and their intelligent, elusive mother.

Even among the relative plenty of Grandmother Margaret's I was a stasher. The reflex reaches even further back to when I was five and my parents became health food zealots. Seeking to address my mother's ailing health and spirit, their conversion from a solid diet of junk food was abrupt. Pretty much overnight all the white stuff I subsisted on—white bread, white sugar, iodised salt in a white plastic dispenser and milk—was rolled into one fearsome signifier, *white death*, and eliminated along with other good stuff like lamb chops, and five-cent mixtures in white paper bags. In their place came foods of child-admonishing intensity. Acrid kelp sprinkled on grated beetroot; carrot and celery salad. Bitter greens and fistfuls of vicious parsley straight from the garden. Sanctimonious brown rice and homemade bread. Only those nasties, dates, for treats.

By day, I stashed the celery moons and beetroot gratings in the pockets of the Liberty print, viyella dresses my mother hand stitched. The crooked hang and brooding palette of these creations bore the stamp of her personality not mine and picked me out from the playground polka dots and daisies. Today, those dusky dresses would be fawned on. Then, I was merely grateful that I could fit half my dinner in their paisley pockets. Come nightfall, I hurled the vegetable matter under my bed where it accumulated like unexploded ordnance.

Unleavened school sandwiches, the subject of much playground disgust, went straight into the convolvulus wilderness at our Waiheke Island front door, right before I entered it after school. My mother swept the vegetable rejects out from under my bed but said nothing. Instead, she restored a semblance of treats to my life. Expensive sticks of dried papaya appeared, only to spear their way into the gully alongside the sandwiches. I liked the dried bananas, little wizened cigars of slightly off intensity, more; less so honeycakes made from tamarillo pulp, honey and coconut and rolled into primitive balls. To these naively misshapen things—no child would stoop to eat them—my father was addicted. He turned a blind eye to the twenty-cent coins I stole from his leather money pouch for the Pie & Jelly Tip Deal at the school canteen. In the same spirit, he retrieved my ditched lunches from the vegetation tip at the front door without comment.

I was a pot-bellied child. Self-contained, sunny-smiled, and furtive as required. My grandmother swore the belly was malnutrition when I arrived at hers. She had her own issues with my parents. Fortunately, these occasioned rescuing their unhappy issue and taking me to live with her.

It was just as well. The discarded celery moons had grown potty-mouthed in the night. *We're going to get you*, and *Shut up bitch*, they swore in nightmare. I woke each night calling for my father. He reliably arrived, stroked my head with big-palmed hand and told me to go back to sleep, before returning to the brass bedstead where he and my mother toiled. I loved him in the mode of an early romantic model, someone you can never get your fill of. It never occurred to me to stop replenishing those ranks of hostile foot soldiers, the celery and beetroot. These fastened my father briefly, nocturnally, to my side.

Towards the end of my stay at the Vinke's, at one of the end-of-year parties we circulate through, more and less like sisters,

Katie gets together with my failed date, strawberry-blond Tom. Almost simultaneously, her younger sister finds herself with boyfriend. Overnight, the bedrooms of the A-frame fill with lovers and closed-door afternoon conferences. The house of solitary musings blooms into a conspiracy of romances. There has always been someone between Katie and me. First it was Ruth. Now, although I don't regret him for his own self, it is Tom.

The sisters sink from sight into sexual intimacy. Their father has returned to claim his wife, morning newspaper and Japanese garden, with brisk vigour. Christmas is in the air. I accompany the sisters on river dates with their boyfriends, the odd one out. The numbers are humiliating, but I shrug them off as best I can. I am passing through and will soon be moving on again. A promise breeding anxiety and hope, evergreen and only slightly shop-soiled.

A footnote called Bill

Julie and her friend Jeanette's competitive interest in Bill intensifies his cachet, even when he is no more than a rumour.

Then I meet him: a legal professional up from Christchurch, staying over at Julie and Lisa's while the former is away on a journalistic assignment. I take keen note of the fact that Bill dresses entirely in bohemian black, the effacing effect of all that monochrome interrupted by an inch or two of forested forearm and pale features under a crown of feathered hair. He reminds me of the urban, chain-smoking left-wingers Aunt Amanda cultivated when I was a child, but stiller.

Bill will be sleeping in the bed where I usually stay on my nights over. I grumble about this to Lisa. Her narrow eyes wreath in smiles. *Maybe you could ask him if he'd share?* She merely shrugs when I opt instead for the foam squab on the living-room floor.

In the stubborn twilight of the street-lit room, the idea of Bill sleeping in Julie's spacious double bed is ever-present, aromatic. After midnight I migrate down the hall. Bill's door is ajar. I hover on the threshold. *OK?* he asks eventually. I fidget. *It's too light in the front room, the streetlight. Would you mind, do you think . . . ?* Bill lifts the sheet. He's got his black T-shirt on. There's something tacit about him, unbroachable.

We lie on our backs, careful not to bump. We're like horse rustlers out on the sheeted plain. Primed, stealth, uncertain, waiting to strike. Or not. Hours pass. Lisa's oversized T-shirt is keeping me modest, just. Bill sleeps the sleep of a man without intentions. Do I have intentions? Not really, but I'm not quite sure about this. I stay awake, trying not to breathe.

In the morning Bill makes me toast and smiles. Bill doesn't have a problem with female moves. Maybe he even likes them. What kind of a man is this?

Little Pete and Blue

Between school's end and my departure for Manaroa, I make a trip to the edge of the city, to Tahuna from whence Eddie Fox and John of Saratoga beckon. No sooner do I arrive, however, than I am driven to seek refuge. So many strange adults, all inducted into the complex hippy codes of which I am novice. Taking shelter in one of the shady sleepouts that map the grounds, I encounter Little Pete and Blue. With long hair caught in a tail, Little Pete is Māori, languid, mild. Blue is Australian, red-haired, hard case—what else? Yet to master the machismo of the older residents, these boys are voluble and bogan, and their clothes are artlessly shabby. I take to them at once.

They are more recognisably working class than the hippies I have met thus far, who have walked away from unfinished degrees or are autodidacts trained in the art of hand-shingling Japanese pagoda roofs. Unlike those white-collar exiles, manual labour carries no exotic charge for Little Pete and Blue. Finding no grounds to mythologise them—they are only a year or two older—I am free to enjoy their company as is.

Despite an open-door policy, visitors are indifferently tolerated at Tahuna. Our low status is apparent when a bunch of blokes dribble into the communal kitchen, where, waiting on the range top kettle, we might as well be invisible. These agrarian throwbacks arrive fresh from the fields, deep in argument about their ailing technology and their horses' shodding. The technology in question is an antique plough. I have sighted this recalcitrantly frail machine: a piece of steam punk before steam punk. Little Pete and Blue are too skittish for hardcore agricultural graft; not inclined, besides. As for me, some divisions of labour in the hippy world are, thankfully, as sexist as elsewhere. As one we melt away.

Back at the dumpy sleepout, we horse around. Me with my outlandish word stock and intermittent airs; Little Pete and Blue with their cocksure and curious. They don't hit on me, or I them. We are just interested enough in each other not to be interested. In the afternoon idle Little Pete fires up a bong and accepts my demurral without comment.

Little Pete and Blue will visit Manaroa when I live there, each drifting ashore on a personal cloud of marijuana smoke. There our differences will settle into indifference. They don't read books. They disappear themselves into a weed haze. Each is without object in the harbour, Manaroa. After an initial hail-fellow-well-met (the hippy hug), I will scorn them.

That summer afternoon at Tahuna is a loophole in time and compatibility, a stay in which we swing our legs off the sleepout mezzanine, stupid with laughter, and incinerate a savannah of time with the magnifying glass of our small talk.

Trouble with shoes

My other visit to Tahuna is less charmed. Without knowing whether she is in residence or not, I plan to visit Jewels. In her absence, I come across a barefoot American with stained toes and the large head of an over-thinker. We get talking. Or rather, he gets talking and I listening. Looking closer, I notice something haunted in his enlarged amber eyes, but by then it is too late: I am caught in Leonard's looping monologue, too sticky with abstraction to extricate myself. Perhaps he is actually making sense and I am too stupid to understand.

After unsuccessful sympathy sex with Leonard I navigate the groves of yellowing bamboo, and unknown sleepouts alone. Who felt sorry for whom?

Eventually, I stumble into Eddie Fox. Installed across from the Welshman, underneath the mezzanine that houses his swag, I take in how bare his shack is of personal traces. We sit cross-legged across a worn rug and, as our back and forth develops, I am conscious of being given audience by straight-backed, black-browed, not-entirely-stable-himself Eddie Fox.

There is a rumour that Eddie once served in the Foreign Legion. Thanks to the hippy aversion to fact checking and the taboo on direct biographical enquiry, this rumour has smouldered, and Eddie Fox's cautionary mystique has grown in a way that he might approve of. Maybe he even started the rumour himself. He's not a Fox for nothing.

As for Leonard, he and his troubles fit into the category of one of those acid cases that fret the edges of the communal scene. Eddie unpacks the LSD burnout scenario with me. His inclination is to sort Leonard out, give him a talking to, a sending off. *Nothing a stint in the army wouldn't fix*, he decides, enjoying his own non-pacific rhetoric, his defiantly-out-of-joint-with-prevailing-mores.

I stick to my humanist non-guns and, feeling heavily complicit in what has passed between me and the haunted American, find myself taking Leonard's side. It is not intervention I am after, but confessional.

From across the rug, and the much greater distance of age, gender, history and inclination, Eddie Fox listens. He is curious, philosophical, and prone to threats of formal violence. His militaristic solutions bring me back to myself. Maybe that was the plan.

Looking down the cloudy glass of the years, I sense Eddie hefting his own undisclosed pain. He carries himself matador-conscious in white shirt and flashing eyeballs, but he lands heavily. His gallantry is slightly off-piste, pissed, nothing quite square or straight about it. His stealth tread and bare feet—we are all routinely barefoot but Eddie Fox more so—fail to conceal a limp and the kind of excruciatingly high arches that have trouble with shoes.

A visit to the doctor

I have made an appointment with a GP. I do not recall where I source his name—in all probability, Nelson's slender Yellow Pages.

After making poor progress with a pelvic examination, the doctor returns to his desk and my newly opened file. *You have vaginismus.* Not much is known about this relatively rare condition, he explains, but in it, an involuntary spasm of the pelvic muscles temporarily seals entrance to the vagina. The causes are thought to be emotional. *When will it go away?* I ask, when he has finished his not-much. I can be sure that these muscular spasms will cease as soon as I have learned to relax, he reassures. A little like *being yourself* for the camera, I think.

My sexual encounters have been occasional and short-lived so far, and I have been dedicated in disregarding the pain that accompanies them. Even so, every time I forge ahead, ignoring the warning signs, intercourse is agonising and penetration near impossible. After each encounter I imagine the next will be easier. It isn't. Now my unconscious sexual dissent has been given a name. Could it be that I don't *want* to have sex? This mortifying question lies unasked.

The thing is, whenever my readiness to live unsupervised or fend for myself does come into question, my insecurity is offset by my verbal facility. In response to the doctor's enquiries I am relaxed about my father's unconventional parenting, and the lack of contact with my mother. I am amusing on the challenges of flatting with adults; modestly confident regarding academic performance. Casual sex I present as the choice I believe it to be.

What I omit is the relative absence of boys my own age with whom to negotiate sex in conditions of relative equality;

the opportunism of older hippy men. I wouldn't know how to begin to describe these murky transactions. I harbour a strong sense of personal responsibility, besides. As I see it, I live a difficult freedom, but it is mine.

What I *am* keenly aware of during my visit to the GP is that, in presenting as an articulate young woman, the interaction flatters both me and the doctor. I am aware of my own performance. In turn, the doctor allows himself to be impressed; it is difficult to intervene on behalf of a patient who seems so in possession of her narrative, however unconventional the narrative is. And besides, what form could his intervention take? I nod earnestly at his suggestions for counselling and take a number I will never call. Then I am released.

Will my child's body ever become a woman's? Will my walled muscles ever relent? I am in dread. And yet, a grain of relief: my body has taken matters into its own hands. There can be no more sex until *I* want and desire it. Grimly, in the privacy of my own mind, I acknowledge this.

In whom can I confide the V word? At Trafalgar Street, Lisa takes the news of my diagnosis with reassuring sangfroid—as one more turn in the complex life of a woman. She makes the remedy sound simple enough. *Slow down*, she half-teases. *Your body is telling you to slow down.* Sitting up and swivelling into profile on the edge of her futon, Lisa begins weaving her hair into two plaits so that she looks like the deft, serious schoolgirl she once was. I have interrupted her afternoon nap. At twice my age, this older woman remains close to her own Glaswegian adolescence. Perhaps this is why she is sometimes able to keep me company as I negotiate the untender traps of mine. Nimble fingers braiding, Lisa talks me unhurriedly through foreplay and clitoral orgasm, those excellent reasons not to rush and even, for a while, to eschew penetrative sex.

Sealords and ladies

In the early new year, following graduation, I sign on as a casual at Sealord fish factory in Port Nelson. This is my quick-fix solution for funding the paint job of the caravan that is to be my new Manaroan home.

I am about to discover that there is nothing casual about the shock of punch-on, punch-off labour, and of 6am starts and 4pm clock-offs. About smoko sirens that signal a choice of either cigarettes on hosed-down concrete dock or tea and slice in the canteen. About the frigid cold store where we paint fish with brown dye to make it appear properly smoked after treating it to a wafting in the smoke chamber. About an ocean of men and women in white overalls, gumboots and those soft filigree cages, hairnets.

At Sealord's I embark on my life-long habit of hanging outside with those commentators on the scene, smokers. Anything to escape the splashdown interior of fish-stink conveyor belts, the freezing hands and crushing monosyllables, and the older women who are in this for life. Out on the concrete apron, a man trapped inside a hairnet makes significant eye contact. He's a natural comedian the size of a kauri tree, and he likes the look of me. The concrete is slippery with too-quick rapport, with my desire not to hurt another's feelings, and his outsize gestures. I know a bit about men and their merry preludes by now, and I'm beginning to know even more about myself. I twinkle back at the kauri tree and maintain my distance.

In the relentless illumination inside, the fluorescent that leaves no place for the imagination to flourish or hide, I am losing sight of my short-term status. Here for the price of a coat of paint, I have fallen into the moment; am trapped inside a science-fiction musical without the musical numbers. Not only do I keep missing the cannery production-line cues—the plastic-gloved micro-order of *this* move before *that* as we women stand evenly spaced along conveyor belts scattered with small glistening corpses—I don't believe in them.

Nothing thus far has prepared me for the totalitarian ontology of the factory universe in which I've fetched up—or the stench. The forty-minute walk from Nile Street where I am staying to the grey lands of Nelson Port delivers me, a vegetarian school-leaver, to fish murder on an industrial scale.

On day six of my employ, a Saturday, I sleep through 6am clock-on. My body knows better than my dutiful self what to do. Later that week, I take the walk to the port a final time to collect my first—and last—yellow pay packet. Inside is just enough cash to purchase two four-litre cans of high gloss, emerald-green exterior paint, a paint tray, roller and wide-gauge brush to cover the blinding aluminium surfaces of my new caravan.

I am Manaroa bound.

PART 3
The Pines, Manaroa

Three houses

A five-minute descent from my father's car-packing-case house, down through the pine belt, across the creek one way, then back again over a felled trunk downstream and you reach my sister's gypsy caravan. Commissioned by my father, it is custom built to picture-book design right down to the pot belly stove and smoking chimney. Grandfather Sam funds it.

The caravan interior is a living disorder of clothes and treasure: the rat's nest of Ratty. My sister detests my father's nickname for her, and it *is* rich coming from him. Growing up in separate households as we have, I am forever behind with her name preferences. *Frida*, *Budi*, *Squirrel*, and *Ribby* or *Ribston* after Beatrix Potter's blue-eyed tabby enjoy their consecutive places in the sun. From the time she can speak, my sister stakes her sovereignty with naming rights. The family legend that, by four, she has decided our parents are stupid is probably no fiction.

For his quarters my father ad libs a sleepout made of a plywood car-packing case, with improvised awning window and door. In a recent life the crate shipped a BMW from Germany. After my father pays a token sum for it in Blenheim, the BMW's giant wrapper is set down on the Island, a grassy slope between two arms of the creek, above Manaroa's farmhouse, the Pines. A bed, the exercise-book diaries, a carton of clothes, and private fruit and honey supplies consume the case's interior real estate. Sitting on its doorstep, alone on his hermetic hill, my father likes to take his morning fruit salad after a few salutes to the sun; cutlery, bowl, and face rinsed in the icy water of the creek, after.

One of the last things my father did before leaving Canvastown was buy an aluminium caravan from some locals who used it to doss down in on rabbiting jaunts. If his eldest daughter was going to join him at the end of her school year, she would need something to sleep in. Ironies multiplied like the ghosts of the former rabbits. My father shelled out a hundred dollars cash and promptly found $110 stowed under the caravan's kapok mattress. He is a pauper who sleeps in a BMW casing; I am a vegetarian about to sleep in a bunny slayer's caravan. (I have finally ceded to family culture and become one—a vegetarian, that is.)

Reached by way of the pine-trunk bridge, my new home is a silver eyesore plonked downstream from my sister's picturesque one. When I visited in the school holidays, a paint job was floated in the communal kitchen. Here I come, a high-gloss emerald can in each hand.

Arrival

I take the long slow walk from the mail boat and pier up the valley to the Pines. My father's lightbulb smile and my knitted sister accompany me. I am ecstatic to be here, to be travelling through the looking glass into life as a Manaroan. It smells of grass and incense, this new life.

The tins of paint bring up the rear by dray. It will take me summer's end into autumn to paint the caravan's ends and the side facing the road. I am stubbornly ungifted. The remaining aluminium face stays as it is, glaring inward across the creek at the main house. It is a case of two evils, the emerald being much louder than anyone anticipated. Fortunately, no one cares much by now.

My ex-rabbiting caravan has a bare-board floor, a wax-spattered kitchen chair and a demolition leadlight hung at one of the two windows that look out onto the road. Despite converting the interior wheel covers to slippery altars by addition of velvet scraps, art nouveau cards and Indian bangles, I am unable to make much impression on the serviceable ugliness of the caravan—inside or out. A strategically placed stone helps me step up and over the raised door's threshold. Once inside, the only place to be is on the platform bed. Erected before my arrival by an obliging hippy carpenter, the bed is so tall I vault into it every night.

Where we gather

Life turns in pre-electrical dim once again for I am in the Pines kitchen, where orphaned chandelier crystals and an unmoored pane of leadlight at the window refract submarine light from the garden. If the farmhouse is a creaky ship rolling on waves of verdure, the kitchen is the galley where we gather to assemble rations. And rations they are. At the heart is a wood-fired range and its living satellite, a bubbling sourdough culture that yeasts the community's bread and chapati supply.

The former quarters of landowners Mick and Edie, who abandoned this pile for another across the fields, the Pines farmhouse comes with a parcel of less-than-arable land and a peppercorn rent. The majority of Manaroans sleep beyond the garden in caravans, sleepouts and even a woodshed, coming to the kitchen first thing to eat, drink, socialise and workshop the business of the day.

While the kitchen is the site of continual human traffic, the rest of the house is becalmed. Off the kitchen is a room the size of a small ballroom that, lacking soft furnishings, refuses domestication. A few guitars stand by awaiting musical visitors and the impromptu parties they bring. Otherwise, it is all bean bags and, ill defence against the chill vast, a cavernous hearth. The shimmy of grain and rattle of turning bicycle spokes provides an alternate soundtrack to C90 cassettes—for a standing bicycle has been ingeniously attached to a wheat grinder in order to produce what flour is needed. We take turns pedalling, grinding cupsful of grain into meal while staring out the grubby panes of the ballroom French doors into the garden. Bush mechanics and Depression-style cooks, routinely conjuring something from nothing much, underwrite our existence.

Resources are alternately bountiful and lean at the Pines. We won't contract scurvy thanks to the abundance of the kitchen garden with its beds of parsley and its tamarillo and lemon trees, but nor is the concept exotic. Some days, I wonder if my sister's childish pot stomach is a sign of malnutrition. Kim, the other small girl on community, has one too.

Am I ventriloquising my grandmother's concern for me when I first arrived, a six-year-old with protuberant belly, at hers? There is anxiety around food and feeding—*how much, how often, the right kind*—across at least three generations of my family. It is tempting to read this as the displacement of fears about other forms of nourishment. As if food were *the* expressive vehicle for comfort and security or the lack thereof; was the only legitimate means of embodying and discussing these things. I am not making a claim for anything unique. In midlife my father takes up the gag about compensatory eating at his own expense—and never seems able to put its modest sadness down. When, at eighteen or nineteen, I hear the Modern Lovers' song 'Hospital', the lines that slay me concern a man who declares he goes *to bakeries all day long / There's a lack of sweetness in my life.*

It is equally true that in my grandmother's Depression childhood, in my parent's health food extremism on Waiheke Island, and now at Manaroa, food is often scarce.

Peaches the Cow is a good milker but the lack of good pasture or credit available to purchase hay limits her supply. For this reason, her calf, Cream, was shipped off young to sister-commune Tahuna. A score of chooks fail to produce their equal number in eggs each week, and what eggs they do lay, the two growing girls and sometime resident boy, Sai, have priority over. Soya beans are the most reliable source of protein, but no one bar my father likes these. Butter, sugar and, occasionally, a block of cheddar arrive on the Tuesday or Friday mail boat from Havelock General Store—when we can afford to order them.

The storeroom is further testament to the exile of luxury. On a good week there might be a sack of wheat, rice, soya beans and oats apiece; some dried pasta; a safe containing a few pounds of butter; and nothing much else. Very occasionally there might be a coveted bag of roasted coffee beans or a few jars of tomato or peach preserves. Not much with which to feed the ten or so core residents, a number that can ebb to four or five in winter but swells, literally, with the tide and whomsoever the mail boat brings in summer. We are often just this side of hungry at the Pines, dining erratically but attentively. Gourmets thrive in the scant for we are time rich; a restricted choice of ingredients only seems to concentrate the communal palate.

Community chest

The storeroom also houses the community chest, whose mythological reputation precedes acquaintance. This huge trunk provides the basis for a revolving shared wardrobe. It is fathomless, the community chest. When our blasted nuclear unit eventually ships from the Floodhouse—and in my case, Nelson—to Manaroa, I am immediately embroiled in the community chest's inexhaustible charms. New stuff seems to manifest there day by day. But only if you dig. Then, it is as if, in upturning the pile, you don't just throw up new combinations but bring new things into being. Magical and kaleidoscopic it is.

Between argyle vests and fringed brocade bedspreads, pilled knits, old-man pin-stripes and forties lapels, there is suddenly something wafty and unguessed-at to be fished out. A rust-coloured dress of post-war crêpe only lightly stained. Or a stiff square of transparent mint organza to drape over afternoon teas we shan't be having.

Once, deep in days of not much, I pluck from the community chest a strapless baby-blue taffeta sheath with a layer of jewel-encrusted lace sculpting the torso. I am an instant teenage bombshell. With nowhere to go in this outlandish borrowed glamour, I take a turn of the Manaroa kitchen garden.

I find Kate's lover Rob crouched in a dirt row, weeding lettuces. A light-boned, often overcast man, Rob is maybe not my best prospect. I clear my throat. Rob looks up. The harsh New Zealand light impales my unlikely vision. I feel like Mae West but without the height, scriptwriter or improvisational talent. I say something idiotic in a phoney voice to signal that I am in on the joke—*Hi, honey* or *Wanna party?*—except that halfway through I fuck it up: swallow and lose the voice. Nor is

Rob a happy object of my attentions. He is so embarrassed he's angry. He mutters, cuts off his stare and returns to weeding. Oh. He thinks I am trying to make a fool of him.

Rob has been making me feel stupid ever since I arrived at Manaroa. He is, above all, a master of refusing to answer questions. *Work it out*, he'll say with a double smile when I enquire into some new procedure or custom. Doesn't he realise that my guileless inanities are mostly intended as entrées to some better, deeper, more rewarding conversation? Not for Rob, small talk. Or dress-ups.

I turn around and go back inside in my taffeta and lace, shamed but not completely dashed. This pale-blue bombshell number is, maybe, just not the dress you wear for an early afternoon tour of the lettuces.

Floor plan

The storeroom opens into a sunroom that runs the width of the house. This glassed-in veranda frames a view of farmland rolling majestically down the valley and into a glimpse of the Sound. In this long afterthought of a room sleeps Dean, a mildly tattooed lady on sabbatical from her street smarts. At six or seven, platinum-blond Kim shares her mother's bed.

She's sexy, Dean, with a tarry voice, lopsided smile, and a gaze that dances with deceptive lightness over the scene. A melancholic, in fact, who has decided not to let it cramp her style. I take to Dean immediately and decide to make her a Venus box as homage. The Venus box is a round papier-mâché trinket box featuring a red fox, twining flowers and a fair bit of my prized tube of silver paint. Dean is a sensuous Taurus to my beauty-worshipping Libra; both ruled by the planet Venus.

Dean is also the only woman at Manaroa who, betraying her urban sensibilities, plucks her eyebrows. In the service of such, she has cut a rectangular chink out of the front window panorama with an offcut of mirror that inserts the inside outside. Mirrors being relatively rare in this household, I seize the opportunity whenever the sunroom is vacant to examine what fragments of my reflection the sliver of glass offers up.

I have recently heard it said that if you can stare directly into your own reflected eyes for half an hour without blinking, your past lives float before you. I'm unsure if it is possible to avoid blinking for so long, and even less sure about the concept of reincarnation. Arcana like this arrive from time to time with the mailboat and its human cargo. The core citizenry wouldn't be caught dead staring into the mirror like this. Convincing myself that the challenge of focus attracts me almost as much as the quixotic project of narratives in the glass, I fail at both.

The storeroom's other egress leads to Bruce's pit. From here the resident stoner emerges late and retreats even later. As far as I know only Bruce's occasional lover Dean—and his absent love Pearl, as alluring and fugitive as her name—ever visit that grotty country. An incidental blessing, then, that Bruce's is one of the only rooms in the house that has retained a functioning door.

Years on an acquaintance comments that until you have mastered the art of getting up before lunch you have not left adolescence. He might have coined the observation for Bruce.

The food of great-aunts

No one holds a regular job and, even if they were so inclined, there are few to be had in this remote corner of the Marlborough Sounds. There is seasonal work at the fisheries, or further afield in Blenheim's orchards. Given the opportunity, everyone participates in the occasional stint of gardening or handy-manning at neighbouring Sounds homesteads and farms. Sometimes I tag along on these group hires. Once to the property of Mary and Denis, who commission annual spring maintenance on their summer holiday cabins. A small work gang takes the mail boat towards French Pass: Kate and Rob, Sylvie, that small, fierce unit Bernadette (also known, fittingly, by her initials, B. Ware), and me. Anticipating light work with plenty of breaks for scones and jam, store-bought fruit cake and luncheon sausage sandwiches, we depart with alacrity. It will be a date with the food of great-aunts from childhood past.

By great-aunts, I refer to those on my father's mother's side. These were the three McKenzie sisters. Grandmother Susan made four. There was Maisie of the peeling pearls and towering loveliness; Isa of the lilac hair and house of shell boxes, carved Chinese trunks and husband Alec, who kept Cuban cigars in a box with Pierrot painted on the inside lid; Elizabeth, more severe. On rare visits my childish appetite was baffled by the food these great aunts disinterred from coronation tins and cupboards. How did you achieve such universal dryness?

Maisie cared little for food or female effects but was impelled by gender and station to go through the motions. The seams of her complexion were peachy with powder, but there was something about the lastborn sister attractively unanchored to the exactions of the material plane. Long-boned and plucky, she had once travelled the world as a war nurse. Eventually, after Elizabeth was widowed and her children left home, Maisie moved in with her elder sister. This, she confided to my father, was like *living with a headmaster*. My father knew what *that* was like. Maisie chose the right person to talk out of school to. Her sense of mischief kept her ageless.

When I was nine or ten, I asked Maisie if I could try on her pearls. She was reluctant and when I lifted the lid on a porcelain dish, I saw why. The pearls, revealed as peeling plastic, found their mirror in the drab room, the single bed with the droopy foliage of a houseplant that has failed to thrive. My encounter with the jewellery box's contents was a blue note that seemed to stand for other humiliations. Maisie saw my regret and was further embarrassed. Then the moment passed. The thing is, Maisie did thrive. She was enterprising, my favourite aunt, someone who knew how to make light, especially with a child.

In the drought of consumables that is Manaroa, the food of great aunts is something to be looked forward to. Our working party is loquacious as we dig and weed garden beds or repaint the trim of the rooms for let. We know that Denis and Mary welcome our presence in their isolated cove as much for the change of conversation partners as anything else. In the evenings we sip sherry in a tiny kitchen whose walls are shingled with Denis's strangely bald paintings.

One brown painting features a wood block with an axe buried in it. Another, a serviceable cup and saucer. Nothing more. A mermaid eyeballs the viewer balefully from a sea of straight-out-of-the-tube blue in a third. The mind glazes over, then returns to the small blunt images in case it missed something. But no, the imagery is stolidly rendered and exactly what it is: the work of a practical joker who winks at us as he sits beneath his homage to cliché. All that is left to do is guess the titles. We shout our replies, and the naming turns to sport. *A Chip Off the Old Block! Not My Cup of Tea! Plenty of Other Fish in the Sea!* Denis thinks it a gas. Several sherries to the wind, we are inclined to agree.

Who owns the buildings?

I am to be paid company for the elderly owner of a summer house down the road from the Pines who wishes to stay a few nights more after her friends have returned to Blenheim. Arriving just before lunch, I think I might like her. I am an admirer of glamour at any age, maybe even more so when the idea takes precedence over the actual. This principle applies to the owner *and* to her villa, which, despite its elegant façade, has fallen to neglect and the settled hostility of empty rooms only occasionally intruded upon by people.

I haven't been here long when, facing off a kitchen stocked with echoes and mouse droppings, I overhear myself referred to as *The Girl* from the next room. *The Girl is making me an omelette*, announces the elderly party in a posh voice on the party line. Her blithe use of the definite article gives her away. I feel my grandmother's blood rising. They come down to class, my relations with this woman, after all.

The Girl doesn't take. Nor does the summer visitor, who decides to head back to Blenheim before nightfall. I had hoped to converse, but under these conditions I have no conversation in me.

There are other Sounds establishments like the Omelette Eater's. Large, draughty, and dust-sheet ghosted for whole seasons at a time, they feature dim wattage and the Anglophiles and colonial relics who still discreetly stock New Zealand in 1980. A post-war austerity persists in décor, provisions and spirit, although sometimes there are grass tennis courts and picnics on the beach with full cutlery sets. Thanks to my parents' potter-friend Maureen, I find myself in a few of these establishments. I'd follow Maureen anywhere. With a shouty, flirty capacity for enjoyment that outshines her drab friends, Maureen is English and, when she remembers to be, a snob.

It is with this statuesque former-blonde that I visit a small colony, interleaved by marriage and birth, that owns a whole bay and its enclosing hills in Kenepuru Sound. Once there, Maureen, who has come equipped with an inflatable air mattress, decides to camp on the rhododendron-dotted lawn, leaving me to the bony rooms of a villa owned by Maureen's spinster friend. After we have erected a canvas fly under the flowering trees, Maureen bounces demonstratively on the mattress. With her robust curves and melancholy air of fun, the scene tweaks a memory of *Carry on Camping*. Granny Margaret once took me to this sex comedy. Misled by the title into thinking the film an adventure story for children, we stayed on anyway, united in smut and hilarity.

They pay a flat annual rate of two hundred dollars for electricity in this insular and wealthy Kenepuru colony, having financed the bulldozing of the road in and the installation of telegraph poles along it. According to Maureen, you can leave the lights on all night. In unsparingly well-lit boredom, I leap at the chance to watch *The Fly* (1958) on the black-and-white television with Maureen's teen son, Geoffrey. My first horror film, in which, thanks to an ingeniously horrible glitch in the teleportation plot—a fly entering the lab booth at the same time as the hero—a species hybrid is born. Caught in a spider web in the film's climax, a tiny, male human head transposed onto a fly's body shrieks *Help me! Help me!* The metallic cries rebound off the empty walls of the living room, piercing me with the expressionistic truth of inter-species incarceration. Geoffrey is sanguine but I take Maureen at her word and lie awake all night transfixed by The Fly's relations buzzing the bright ceiling bulb. If I could only pluck up the courage to pull the light cord.

The next day brings tennis, muted conservative politics and talk of accounts. I keep my grandmother's red politics to myself. No one thinks to ask a sixteen-year-old girl, anyway, but I am more interested in the accounting than I appear. How does their world *work*, I wonder, surveying the dowdy money. *Exploitation*, I hear my grandmother hiss.

Thirty years on, squinting up into downtown Sydney's skyline, my father asks, *Who owns the buildings?* Without waiting for the reply (*corporations*), his mind moves swiftly on to the next meal. Like my father, I am interested in how people set themselves up, and then not. We are an impulsive people and not players of the long game, unless you count the art game, which those who own the buildings mostly don't.

At work and play

For the most part the Manaroans practise the law of divine manifestation, running low-income lives on this article of faith. The eschewal of material accumulation and ambition is a practice so fundamental there is no need even to discuss it. Miraculously, for none of us are religious, divine manifestation holds. It helps that the ask is modest.

Work isn't rostered at Manaroa but takes place as a result of informal murmurs or by independent initiative. Elevated to an ethos, this haphazard arrangement is the rule, and seems to work for the basics and a few more elevated projects besides. The more responsible chafe, my father among them, but the consensus is stronger. This way, no one's autonomy is infracted, but nor does efficiency thrive in our midst. Collectivism is a hazy ideal that none knows quite how to enact.

For some, the day begins early with milking Peaches the Cow. She can be moody and restive—likes to run a new milker off along the fence line on the way to the milking shed and, once there, step on their toes. Protesting your technique, she will lift her tail and defecate close to the pail. The experienced know to wear gumboots or closed-toe shoes. In my case, these don't help; between feed-paddock and shed, Peaches roughly establishes rank. I will not be among the milking crew at first or last light.

Instead I attempt hand-churning the cream skimmed off the top of Peaches's milk in an antique wooden churn with a metal arm. Laborious and boring. Alternatively, you can decant the cream into an Agee jar and, with a wearisome amount of wrist action, transform it into a greasy nugget of pale-yellow solid floating in liquid. I experiment with rolling the jar down the hill at the foot of the kitchen garden instead. The cream doesn't turn. When we can afford it, we eat store butter.

Waiting for Lenny the Horse to shit so you can scoop it up and manure a sapling further trips the absurd. The rejected farming land that we lease, The Land, is almost solid clay. Our subsistence diet is enriched by whatever we grow, and the community gardening project is strenuous but dedicated, giving manure high status.

In general, mundane chores are made epic by the absence of labour-saving devices that became commonplace decades ago. Washing clothes, for instance, is a half-day enterprise that involves splitting firewood to heat the copper in its shed. After simmering the laundry for a few hours, you transfer it to one of two concrete sinks and drag your clothes or sheets repetitively over the metal ridges of another early-twentieth-century prop, a washboard. No one can bear to undertake such toil more than once a month, and so we go smelly.

Taking a bath is equally daunting, involving step one and two of the copper process, then transfer of the steaming contents, bucket by bucket, down the garden slope to the bathroom. We Floodhouse people are used to that.

Gardening in the nude is another tenet of community life. It can be blissfully hot in the valley. We don't wear sunblock, though, for most of us have spent New Zealand childhoods crisping our complexions pink, red and brown and see no reason to stop. We have not yet learned to be wary of the sun. I engage in degrees of nudity as it suits. It's surprisingly easy once you begin. The view of burnished bodies is a reliable pleasure and, thanks to the everydayness of it all, there is no awkward voyeurism at work.

Private building projects also simmer in our midst. There is an unusually high proportion of gifted carpenters and even cabinetmakers here. Almost as many as there are guitar players and university dropouts.

Without the distractions and obligations of capital—shopping, for instance—and decades before the Internet and social media, there is ample time for reading. Our sunroom library, replenished by visitors, features novels by Gabriel García Márquez, for whom a feverish appetite is sweeping the hippy world. There are Hermann Hesse, Tom Wolfe, Erica

Jong and, need I say, Kahlil Gibran's *The Prophet*. A much-thumbed copy of Simone de Beauvoir's *The Second Sex*, with the second half missing as if someone has sliced the book in half like a loaf of bread and consumed one end. Perhaps the reader was lying in bed and found it too heavy to hold aloft. The book's incompleteness intrigues me and forms a barrier I do not overcome even though I haul the truncated tome off to my caravan on several occasions.

You will also find a text or two on Sufism, the Kundalini, and a much-consulted *I Ching or Book of Changes*, with foreword by Carl Jung, on the shelves. If you wish to throw the I Ching coins, in order to obtain a hexagram for interpretation, you must apply to Sylvie, who keeps a personal set, with the distinctive square hole in the centre of the coin, in a silk pouch in her caravan. Otherwise, three ten-cent pieces will do. In equally high rotation is the ephemeris of astronomical data listing a century of night skies, a stack of supplementary star charts and a small collection of interpretative astrology texts. Again, Sylvie keeps a pad of templates for plotting birth charts. There are a number of amateur astrologers here.

My sister and I draw; my father keeps his copious diaries. Faced with no school and a surfeit of days, I begin an illustrated diary myself, a commission from the newly opened Women's Gallery in Wellington. I no longer recall how I come by that invitation. Anointing the pages with Duc de Berry blue and silver paint, I wonder whether this cosmic aspect will be out of sync with the gallery's more worldly feminist agendas. Unsure how to cut myself to their honouring cloth, on I go.

Bar my family, there are no other self-identifying artists or writers here. *Too much manual labour deadens the brain*, my father glosses.

Talk

Whatever my father thinks, the kitchen talk is intriguing. It is epigrammatic. Cynical. Minimalist. Cool. Stoner talk, one of the subgroups, is sparser still. Rich in non sequitur, absurdity and in-jokes, interrupted by sudden collision with the icebergs of silence. I pay the silences close heed. They are intimidating, and frequently boring, too. The workaday talk of method, process and technologies to hand, I tune out.

What we don't talk about is almost as important as what we do. 1980 is in the second term of Robert Muldoon's National prime ministership and, for the handful of farmers down the bay, Muldoon is their man. Since he came to power in 1975, disdain for Piggy Muldoon and his populist policies had been set to a low roiling boil at my grandmother's. Up on the hill at the Pines, Muldoon's existence, like that of the entire political establishment, is forgotten. We might as well live in a snow globe given our insulation from current affairs.

A late, idealistic addition to the core residents, my father is early disappointed in Manaroan talk. It is left to visiting musicians, to Claire's expressive garden, and to the unconstrained qualities of light and sky to express lyrical feeling. These notwithstanding, my father has moved here in hopes of imaginative conversation. Evenings and afternoons between his four car-case walls, he complains about the nihilist and anti-intellectual undertow that drags on the kitchen scene, attributing the former to too much dope and the latter to an aggressive strain of deadhead provincialism, mostly male. I have encountered the sneering in the kitchen, and the tacit censorship it enforces, too. It makes me shy to speak up, encouraging me to sharpen my tools of observation more than I might otherwise choose. There is no one my own age to cut loose with.

In an effort to boost expressivity and the communication arts my father decides to write an adult puppet show. This is a rebooted, reflexive adaptation of *Punch and Judy* in which the adaptor takes his revenge on wife-beaters, the patriarchy and his headmaster father. Manned by the lumpy papier-mâché glove puppets my father likes to knock out and staged in an improvised booth in the main house's ballroom, the show is a hit with the culturally starved masses. Us. My father calls on a woman who lives across the water to co-work the hand puppets. Michelle has an oddball sense of humour, is more art school than hippy, and is, all-importantly, female. This trifecta adds value to my father's shows.

Inspired by the success of his and Michelle's *Punch and Judy*, my father writes a live-action play: a satire on the core Manaroans, cast from within our midst. Most memorable are the cross-dressing blokes—in particular Hooki, a conservative but wistful macho who takes to dresses and pearls with surprising flair. Doug, Claire and Rob also make compelling debuts. As a rule, the more recessive the human, the more stage daring they reveal. I am the exception. Who wants to be cast in their father's weirdness?

And the play is truly weird. Competing with the amateur players and their cross-dressing flare are the script's strange one-liners: *Your eyes are like puddles. I'd like to ride my bike through those puddles*, one onstage flirt says to another. My father's queasy sexual humour and its surreal comment on the Manaroan scene is such a success that his plays, as fast as he can write them, animate the afternoon paddocks where they are staged over the summer months. The commune has found its narrator for a season.

The sheep pause in their grazing to look on at these line-trumpeting humans but not for long.

The Land

There is another kind of talk at Manaroa, as imaginative as any my father could wish for. This is the future-talk of what can be made from the land leased from Mick and Edie. The projected architectural designs of the main community building with library, the feijoa and apricot orchard interspersed with gardens, the beehives and the small private retreats are minutely debated over long months. Manaroa's limited resources—bare hands and backs, demolition timber from Christchurch and Blenheim and the advanced carpentry skills of a few—are no object to the collective dreaming.

Plans drawn up by Rob are heavily annotated, precisely redrawn and closely guarded by the former draughtsman. Unscrolled in the kitchen, these are the subject of long and tedious interrogation by Bruce and his contrarian expertise. These men love an argument. Rob crackles with energy, cunning and pique. Stoner Bruce has got time, more time than the rest of us. It is more rewarding to go dig a deep bed for the equally mythical asparagus or to plant aquilegias with Sylvie.

Eventually talk can postpone action no more, and a raw cut is bulldozed with borrowed machinery across the Land's scrubby tract. This road will provide access to the main-house site, linking, as it climbs and dips, the previously cleared dirt paths that snake the foothills. Dotted with netted fruit-tree seedlings, these tracks lead to newly turned vegetable beds obscured by bracken and chicken wire. The possums are rapacious. Closer to the main-house site, the paths deliver one to cleared patches of clay set aside to erect the sleepout of this or that resident's dreams.

Thanks to the new road, one or other of us will visit the Land at least every other day to clear bracken; break in, water and tend garden plots; or pour foundations and work on the framework of the main building. Makeshift crews of builders evolve in spurts. In propitious times the ranks are swelled by three brothers who come by water across the Sounds from Saratoga and Tahuna. The growing main-house frame rings with hammers and climbing workers.

On other days, Manaroa is no more than a congregation of moody individualists on whom the tedium of routine, conflicting methodologies and egos, the fierce climate, poor soil and the lack of funds take their toll. The humans are not the only ones. The feijoa saplings struggle to find purchase in the clay and wind. Sometimes I meet someone with a wheelbarrow and spade or a sickle on these paths. Sometimes I don't. Alone, I find myself in a dauntingly inhospitable region, either parched or caked with ochre mud depending on recent rainfall, ever scratchy with low-rise bracken. Privately, I find the place vision-proof. Only the ribboning call of the buff-bellied pipit moves me. I long to find its nest of speckled eggs in the spiky fronds.

Erected, the declamatory skeleton of the building remains just so for over a year, a promissory note that may or may not be fulfilled. Even I stand back to admire the massive arched window frames. These beautifully jointed and weathered settings bookend the east and west faces, portals to a visionary time and place. They have been salvaged from a church in Christchurch, then driven up the island in the truck of a susceptible demolition-yard owner—a *straight* no less—who, for his efforts, is felled by a migraine as soon as his precious cargo is unloaded. Sweet-talked on the journey by Kate, and maybe even Rob, Bert lies with a damp tea towel over his eyes in the darkened room off the kitchen for a weekend, then, as soon as he can stand, drives back down the island to work. Even more than the ex-church loot, it is this vulnerable and stoical straight who makes the biggest impression on me. I take him tea.

A season on, in an especially vituperative edition of the gale force winds that ricochet around the Sounds, the shivering grandiosity that is the main house and library frame dismantles overnight, demolition planks demolishing. Once achieved the frame's violent demise registers as a fait accompli. But this is far ahead, in a time when I too will be gone.

A cup of tea

Common or garden desires are the hardest to satisfy at the Pines. If it is a cup of tea you crave, you must first light the wood range. Rain or shine, winter or summer, this is how it is. On a good day this means reaching into the kindling box alongside the range, followed by a short walk around the front of the house to the firewood stack for bigger cuts. Hopefully, the mānuka or demolition offcuts stacked here are dry, but in the rainy climate of the Sounds this is not a given. If the wood is wet or damp, your fire will be smoky and despondent, catch and suffocate. You will crouch at the firebox blowing in the range's black ear, teasing and cursing reluctant fire into being.

On a bad day, one of those days when lack of community on the commune is evident, the kindling box is empty and the outdoor stack exhausted. Not only this, but you are the only one to feel the problem sufficiently to act. Bruce is locked into sofa-place with bong. The most likely of all to reach for a cup of tea, Claire, is still at it, hands thrust deep in the black-crumbed soil.

If you want tea badly enough there is nothing for it but a trip to the Land. Crossing Mick's sheep-dotted pasture and slashing your way through the bracken off the bulldozed main track, you must select then fell one of the runtier mānuka with your axe. A twenty-minute return hike to the Pines, tree dragging behind, sees you at the sawhorse below the pine belt. The saw is stowed in the woodshed, which also accommodates a sleeping loft. Now it is up to you to reduce your culled mānuka into firebox lengths.

After this you must apply to the graces of a wily stove damper that never cooperates without first choking the ceiling in smoke. The good news is that Manaroa is never short a packet of Bushell's finest. The larder may be bare of butter but never tea. From here it is a waiting game. The iron range top is notoriously slow to heat.

On a bad day it might be a half-day action to bring the kettle to whistling. That is how it is. On such a day I won't graduate above hopeful kitchen lurker. I can split kindling. Felling a small tree is another matter.

Telecommunications

The making or taking of a phone call is no less a pilgrimage. This time you set off in the other direction, towards Mick and Edie's farmhouse. Another rural dump, thicketed by near-impenetrable bamboo and watched over by a trio of paranoid farm dogs, this one is better-secreted than ours. Approaching the garden gate, one waits for Mick to appear. Short, battered and staunch, the landowner's lips winch into a trollish grin as he beats safe passage through the undergrowth and dogs. It is a bit like approaching Baba Yaga's house; chicken leg foundations would not go amiss. In fact, the chooks are all inside, mixing it with Edie's trousered legs under the kitchen table oilcloth.

Thanks to the generator, Edie's kitchen is flooded with yellow light. Thick with dog hair and mutton fumes, too. Tall-stemmed with flyaway white hair in a bun, dressed like a man, Edie is the grace note. Her understated courtesy, bracing. Addicted to cryptic crosswords, Edie's utterance is a lateral clue to conversation; I am always straining to catch its tail. But when, depending on the nature or severity of the call and other unseen local factors, tea is in the offering, Edie emerges from behind her table-station to reach down the biscuit tin. It is only then that her polio-stiff leg is revealed.

Mick and Edie's phone is attached to the kitchen wall near the doorway of a newspaper-stacked lounge. It is here that Edie retreats with her crossword in order to afford everyone a measure of privacy. Today, I have come to receive a pre-arranged call from my former Wellington Girls' form teacher, Diane McCarthy. Pre-arranged means that Diane has looked up a Manaroa number—any Manaroa number—and, locating one, dialled it. There are only a few phones in the bay. Perhaps she calls two or three farms before she receives instructions on reaching the Pines via Mick and Edie. From there, she and Mick set another time to call. After this Mick is impelled west over his fields to deliver her message.

At the appointed hour, Diane calls and there I am, sitting at Edie's kitchen table, eating a biscuit under the fly strips. I cannot fail to miss the semaphored significance of the occasion. It must be important. And it is. Would I like to come and live with her and her husband Chris?

This is the teacher who once sent me notes from two seats down when a student teacher was taking her class, out-trumping me in schoolgirl moves. Warmed as I once was by this irreverent woman's attention, I have not seen her since I left my grandmother's, and her offer misjudges the degree of independence I feel two years on. I left home too long ago to live in anyone else's family, even one as progressive and economically sound as Diane's. It is too late for me to acquire a surrogate mother.

I imagine Diane hatching the plan at the dinner table, the way it would have caught her inflammable imagination. At Edie's Bakelite receiver, voice rising half an octave in my eagerness to please, I can do nothing but disappoint. I don't want to live at Diane's. I troop back to the Pines, crestfallen. The visitation of others' affections can be a sudden and unpredictable thing.

Economics

There is fallout from Diane's stellar gesture, which, in turn, sheds light on the delicate social engineering of the Pines set-up. It turns out that Diane made her call from a friend's house where she was on holiday. Long after her visit ends, her hosts receive their telephone bill and are dismayed by one inexplicable and expensive item: a toll call to Manaroa in the Pelorus Sound. Diane's friend thinks to solve the matter by refusing payment; the phone company by retrospectively reversing the charge to the receiving account. Mick takes another trudge to the Pines. Payment falls to my privately cursing father. A toll call! Who makes those but in case of death or emergency?

Diane, of course, knows nothing of this chain of relayed charges whose mechanism proceeds so much more slowly but inexorably than her brilliant phone call.

After Mick's visit, a sense of transgression, loss of face and anxiety about provoking the ire of our landlord mushroom-clouds in the Pines kitchen. The fall-out hinges on that taboo subject, money. Specifically, debt. The matter of economics is further pressing in the case of my father, who balances with difficulty the fortnightly welfare cheque for solo parents. Tenant insecurity about alienating Mick and Edie, who have swum against the conservative tide of their neighbours in enabling hippy ratbags to set up house in the valley, is another factor.

Kate, who has more public front than anyone else on the commune, is self-appointed ambassador across the fields. At pains to counter our image as ne'er-do-wells, manifold in charm at Edie's table, Kate returns to report a definite cooling. In the wake of our break in decorum, she advises it will be a while before anyone can use Mick and Edie's phone.

This means no more calls to Havelock the day before the mailboat for an emergency fix of butter or tea, or the Drum tobacco that so many are hooked on. We'll have to get organised and order by mailbag, penning a note to the store for Tuesday's run and receiving the fruits by Friday's boat.

And so it goes just as Kate has predicted. After my father's harassed payment of the reversed toll call, a cool-off period ensues in which we forsake the trip across the fields to Mick and Edie's begrimed connection with the modern world.

Windfalls

Kate hitches the shafts of the dray to Lenny the Horse with Kim or my sister standing in back and, if the tide is right and we've wind of a seaweed-strewn beach, drives to the bay. As fertiliser for the kitchen garden and the Land's arid clay soil, seaweed is much prized. I follow the dray down the wind-whipped road as it stakes a path between paddocks, amphitheatre of hills and mirror-bright sky. Down to the pier where the mail boat draws in.

The mail boat's two visits are the events by which we measure the Manaroa week. The arrival of the locked canvas mailbag, and the steady trickle of unannounced visitors with it, ensures letters and news, friends and strangers. A box of groceries ordered by outgoing mailbag from the Havelock store might be on it or, from further afield, a sack of brewer's yeast for our breakfast chapatis. When Phil Martin travels south from Manaroa for a stint as chef at the Dux de Lux café in Christchurch, he posts back Red Cross parcels of coffee, cheese and chocolate. Mail boat windfalls.

Sometimes Phil himself turns up by sea. Phil is lean as an Anglepoise lamp and as specific. When he's in residence up the slope from my sister's, his caravan is stocked with musical instruments, novels or a volume of Rumi's poems, a kettle and kindling for the pot belly stove. He seems to know how to live, while the rest of us are merely making a pass at it.

The alchemy of mail boat arrivals is unpredictable. We dread a bludger and embrace those who arrive with offerings, energetic or edible. None are ever turned away. Once on my watch the mail boat yields Pearl and, simultaneously, my best friend from another life, Ingrid. I haven't seen or spoken to her for two years, but Ingrid arrives in the all-weather black oilskin of a Wellington childhood. She is as good as a relative, Ingrid—sunnier, despite the oilskin, than my actual ones.

Bruce's lover Pearl is legendary. Standing in the garden, among orange calendula and blue-star borage, Kate solemnly confides that Pearl's beauty is of the classic kind. This means that it will endure, unlike whatever minor gifts the other women of Manaroa possess. Kate is uncharacteristically diffident before her vision of Pearl. It comes down to cheekbones. Impressed by her categorical certainty, I await the evidence.

Pearl alights on the pier, cheekbones spattered with spray and freckles, laughing at everything and nothing as only the physically blessed can. She is wearing something carelessly frail that catches the wind's attention and enhances her haptic attraction. It strikes me that Pearl must always be in motion. Ingrid is already caught in Pearl's sweep and remains so for the visit's duration. It's mutual. In Ingrid's company Pearl is a girl again, and vice versa. There's tickling in the kitchen. Jealous, I keep to myself. The cheekbones are overestimated, I think.

Flickering through the farmhouse, amiable, negligent Pearl is scintillatingly unable to settle. Her infant son, cherubic snot-nosed Jarrah, flutters in her wake. An albino moth to the flame of his mother's social butterfly. Reared on a diet of charm and elusiveness, Jarrah crawls into my lap with a hunger for affection mixed, confusingly, with the free-form sexuality of the under-five.

I wish to be both like Pearl and not. She has the appearance of someone about to slip loose from something. Her expiring peach acetate slip, straps at half-mast and worn as a dress. Early motherhood. Her son. Lover Bruce—who is enthusiastic for Pearl in a way that goes against the grain of his reliable sarcasm. Observing Pearl's animation peak in Bruce's company, I get the feeling of something compensatory afoot. Bruce's snaggle-toothed grin suggests that he is not kidding himself all that well about Pearl. She won't stay—even I can see that.

I am Pearl's witness but, young and unforgiving, I fail to credit her own relative youth. Twenty-four at most, she's only just slipped off girlhood, and her body language and her relationship to Jarrah and to Bruce say that she has done so incompletely and with reluctance. Nor do I credit the other twenty-something Manaroans with being in like formation. To my adolescent eye they are definitive. It doesn't occur to me that, like my own, Pearl's brain may be still forming.

Suddhas, then Sharon

Suddhas comes and goes with the tides, and is, as far as I know, the sole Rajneeshee to visit Manaroa. From our remote vantage we follow with bemused tolerance the dye-pot transformations of the Rajneeshee from orange to wine via a lilac aside. We have little truck with organised religion—of any kind.

Frankly, I think the Orange People are on the disorganised side. Nor am I interested in spiritual practices that preach separation from the world. I am too young to transcend the world—*any world*—thanks. Suddhas is the right side of twenty and, despite the black-and-white photo-locket of Bhagwan bumping on his saffron chest, he wears his spiritual affiliations lightly. Not a word of proselytising passes his lips. The Orange People are famously cool like that.

When I encounter him in the Manaroa garden, gaze mottled as a river-stone and engaged with something just beyond my own, I hope for a few drops of small talk that might lead elsewhere. Suddhas behaves as if the years he has on me are light years. Willing to give him the benefit of the doubt, I focus on the seamless colour of him. Right down to his umber-freckled arms and sea-faring ginger hair. It's funny how compelling such things can be.

It's not until he plays a travelling set of bongos, eyes closed, on a patch of hillside that I decide that elegant, airy Suddhas, of the superb arms, might be vain. *Bongos.* Adolescent cynicism successfully engaged I shift my attentions elsewhere.

Sharon Spratt zooms in on her Ducati in creaking leathers. I have no idea how she has found me. Sharon was barely older than the sixth-form PE students when she turned up as a student teacher at Nelson Girls' and made a habit of engaging me before or after class. That is how she found out that I flatted and my father lived on a commune. Clean-cut and athletic, blond hair in two straight wings, Sharon appeared straight from central casting. For all that, doubts about joining the hierarchies of a girls' college swirled and coalesced in her talk. A questing, anti-authoritarian streak camouflaged by cordiality—this description might have applied to either of us. Although I was five feet tall and a studied failure at PE, she picked me as a kindred spirit. I had occasionally befriended my elders as a child, usually over books. This one befriended me.

Now she is at Manaroa I am flattered and unsure what to do with Sharon Spratt. She sleeps in Doug's caravan—he's away working on the boats—and tools about with me during the day collecting horse manure, chopping kindling, lighting the range for a pot of tea. I think she is making a recce of possibility. If so, she has come to the right place. Possibility is what we dine on here. I draw up Sharon's astrology chart—Sun in Cancer—and we knock about her angles, sextiles, trines and squares. She is wondering what to do next with her life. Briefly, I am her mirror.

I watch to see if she will pounce on one of the men or they her. But she is aloof, and to the natives, I think she must appear as straight as her brand-new, matching leathers. How must she see their downbeat? Grotty and lacking in vision, probably. When Doug shows up unexpectedly in the small hours to reclaim his bed, Sharon is discreet about the night moves. Next morning, I find her innuendo-proof and rumpled from wandering the landscape till dawn. She has not wavered even for Doug. When she climbs back on the Ducati, I am sorry to see her go. Relieved, too, to be released from her restless regard and back into the muddy set of ineffables that is Manaroa.

Loyalties

It is a wet winter's evening when Mick arrives at our kitchen door with torch and tersely mumbled appeal. With our numbers reduced to a seasonal low, I am one of the entire population of four or five who follow Mick over rumpled paddocks in the rapidly closing pitch. Without the ambient light throw of the city night sky, it really is black. Up behind his and Edie's farmhouse, Mick's torch illuminates a muddy slip in the steep pasture. There, the white of a heifer's eye connects with our chorus of kerosene lanterns.

The stranded cow makes a concerted effort to stand and fails. Her stumbles make clear how much she welcomes her loyal human's return—and that she has broken a leg in her fall. As she flails in the shadowy lights, it becomes evident that she is also pregnant. I have been afraid of monosyllabic Mick till now, the reek of beef bones boiling in kerosene tin over gas burner in his bamboo-encircled compound fuelling my foreboding. Mick's cow humanises him. As we watch her enact a desperate greeting it occurs to me—*these two know each other.*

A few hours pass before Mick signals that we should give up scrambling in and out of the pit to push and pull at the heifer. Unceasing rain has made an improbable ascent, slick with further slippage, impossible. Laying her sweating muzzle down, the pregnant cow thinks so too.

That clinches it. Mick climbs back down, and we begin again, wiping muddy hands on greasy oilskins in hope of better purchase. Then a breakthrough in luck and improvised technology. A combination of makeshift winch, a blanket sling, and the heifer becoming too exhausted to get in her own way or ours, enables us to hoist her out.

Lanterns aloft, we make our way back across midnight fields, neighbourly relations—or just as importantly, our perception of these—restored.

The lipstick

My uncle David visits without my cousins but with his new girlfriend, a bookseller. It is she who has the distinction of becoming the first and last woman ever to wear red—or any other colour—lipstick at the Pines. They stay in the room off the ballroom that we reserve for guests, where Bert the demolition man stayed. A room with an east-facing window, a double bed with crochet granny-blanket, and cobweb-sketched walls. The morning after she arrives, the bookseller applies to me, sotto voce, in the kitchen. I accompany her to the slice of mirror in the miserabilist afterthought of a bathroom that the entire commune shares.

I can see that the little stick of roll-on glamour she wields is a talisman of the life from whence the urban bookseller comes and to which she will return on the next mail boat; that the red lipstick is a panic button in the face of unforeseen levels of the domestic abject. Even so, she is sociably ironic about her next requirement. Her period has come early, do I have tampons too? Exposed in self-inflicted rural poverty, I am happy to normalise relations. Yes, I do.

As for the red lipstick in ridged gold tube, I regard it with admiration but as if from a great distance. The bookseller invites me to try. Confronted with my coloured-in reflection, my expression settles into the fatally unsure. Scarlet lips make me a child in dress-up but without the zest.

Seventeen

The night I turn seventeen I shimmy into Ruth's mother's silk georgette wedding dress. Clinging to whomsoever can wriggle it over their head, the effect is reliably transforming, but tonight the dress is wearing me rather than I it. It is late and I am sitting in a sooty club chair with a novel and a handful of gloomy stoners—Bruce, Doug and Rob—for company. We have eaten the carob birthday cake with blue borage flowers winkling in the icing, and the sensible have departed into the cold spring darkness for their beds.

As the remaining company recedes into itself, I brood on the dress's lack of explicit effect. *Going flirty fishing*, the old Greek female tailor who will one day sew dresses for me might call this kind of lightly experimental foray. I don't know which is worse: the room's averted attention or the indiscreet stare that never arrives.

There is the tacit understanding that, among those who live so close, unchecked promiscuity would destroy what fragile equilibrium we have. More specifically, I am visibly the daughter of a father who lives on community. The indifference is mutual, actually, but these are lonely satisfactions. Where are the boys my own age? Not on rural communes, that's for sure. Marooned in fabulousness, I take myself off to bed.

Manaroa isn't sleazy. No beers, glosses Doug sagely when I wonder aloud in years to come at the relative sexual restraint of the community. *Gentleness is effects of beer*, observes drunken clerk Turkey of a usually ill-tempered co-worker in Herman Melville's 'Bartleby'. A favourite story of mine and a favourite line. The opposite holds at Manaroa. Gentleness is effects of no beer. The near-absolute absence of alcohol—not an outlet in miles and no money to buy it even if there was—is a factor. On a single occasion the community gathers to stamp sacks of cherries in the bathtub for wine. The merry queue to stamp, our deliriously ruby feet-to-thighs are an occasion. The fermented product, not so much.

Morning finds me in the shipwrecked vast off the kitchen. Sylvie sweeps while I engage in the pointless shifting of shabby textiles to make the place feel more like home and less like a desecrated ballroom. Doug is there too, smoking a rollie while riding the standing bike attached to the grinder in order to mill flour for his breakfast chapati. Sai careens in. Named after an Indian yogi by his solo mother, Sai is a handsome child of eight or so with a wide smile and a strikingly sober stillness at the centre of his energetic storm. You never know what this stillness might produce, but Sai's intelligence, and the palpable stress of possessing it, is a force. His jet eyes take in first me, then Doug going nowhere on the standing bike. *Did Doug rake Miro last night?* Sai demands of Sylvie.

I have no idea what to do with the furrow the verb ploughs through my brain, with Sai's projection of the casual violence of adult relations, or Doug's embarrassing proximity. There's something cruel and sexist in Sai's formulation. Where did *that* come from? Perhaps from Lex, several teeth missing in a perpetual grin, who passed through recently and was a source of casually vulgar language of the kind you don't otherwise hear here. The lightning rod intuition, especially when it comes to the undercurrents and atmospheres of sexuality, is Sai's own. I *do* have a crush on Doug, but these accusations are of a different order.

As I go, I hear Sylvie attempt a mild, chiding pass at Sai's hand-grenade language, a pass that fails to deconstruct his surprisingly angry view of adult sexual relations. Years down the track I wonder about the nature of this small boy's experience. At the time my own shame is too great to think of anyone else.

Honeydew

The Thompson twins step off the mail boat in the twinned guise of 'Kubla Khan': *For he on honey-dew hath fed, / And drunk the milk of Paradise.* With their peachy complexions, airs and Dürer-wavy centre-parted hair, the Thompson twins do look as if they may have dined on honeydew. *His flashing eyes, his floating hair!*

Their twin sets of eyes are mesmeric green with lucidly delineated spokes that resemble the faces of clocks. I am happy to stare into these time devices, while their owners' minds tick over but slowly, for Tim and Leo are as identical as Hergé's detective twins, Thomson and Thompson, and maybe just as artless. As they aren't much given to talk, it is possible to postpone this realisation for a while—and then, looks ensure them magnetic passage through our world.

Tim and Leo float, indistinguishably, around the Pines for the term between Tuesday's and Friday's mail boat service. Just long enough to discover they are not much older than me. That Tim is friendly, and maybe as lonely as I. And that Leo, hardened into the style of man he will become, is remote. I look hopefully upon the twin I am intermittently able to recognise as Tim. When he offers me a massage, a commonplace enough invitation, I glow with nerves and the pleasure of being singled out.

Tim's lack of conversation incites in me the inverse: the kind of sentences that die an early death from overcomplications. All the way to my caravan, I perform CPR on these ailing monologues. Cloudless as the sky, Tim seems not to notice. Once inside, in the absence of anywhere to conduct small talk and the absence of small talk to be conducted, Tim and I make for the raised platform that is my bed.

Tim has brought along his massage oil. Not wishing to appear inexperienced, I take off my top. Tim takes off everything. Short like me, neatly made, his lion's mane is the thing. I follow suit. Is the moment erotic? Not really. There has been no prelude, no flirting. And, anyway, the prevailing casualness around nudity blankets the erotic in everydayness. There's no denying the ambiguousness of the moment, though. What are we here for exactly? I am not sure.

I lie on my front. Sitting on my bum, Tim spreads warm hands on my lower back. Face to one side on the pillow, I turn with thought. I don't have time to feel much. Then I do. It takes a moment or two to realise that Tim has just had a significant moment on my back. Its insignificance is striking. The massage is over before it has begun.

No one wears harem pants on the commune, but the Thompson twins do. They're hippies from another planet.

Tim tucks himself into his drawstring pants and passes my grandmother's towel. This lonely gesture of acknowledgement is poignant. There is something missing in Tim: the connection of sexuality to reciprocity, I guess. Packing our absent selves away, I catch sight of his stubby, uncomprehending hands and feel at once soiled and sorry for both of us.

Tamarillo Brillo

The cupboard is bare, and we have been on rations for days. Unsure of when the lean times will end, or what relief the mail boat will deliver, we subsist on chapatis and tea. The last-resort sack of soya beans emerges from purdah in the storeroom. Contrary to legend, I have rarely met a hippy who enjoys soya beans. Kim and my sister hang obsessively around the stove in case of further developments, their childish pot bellies cause for speculation once again. Are they ballooning towards malnutrition?

Relief comes from an unexpected quarter. When Bruce breaks his stoned monolith stance on the sofa the results can be spectacular. Long ago, he tells me, in rare confessional, he sailed from Glasgow around the world as a cook serving in the galley of a merchant ship. I don't get much more than this. Bruce operates in stoned time in which verbal ellipses yawn. Even so, this slip of biography conjures classic maritime romance. *He ran away to sea.*

These days, unlike his former industrialised self, Bruce cooks barefoot, moving lightly on long, expressive feet. Mast-tall, he has retained the fleet gestures and dexterous moves of his seafaring self, recasting the Pines kitchen in memory of the galley. Whatever you think of his lackadaisical grooming or nasty wit, Bruce in action at the bench, tea towel serving as makeshift apron, is good to watch. Matted grey wool trousers, ending well short of bony ankles, only enhance the effect. With fair goatee and sharp, wonky teeth when he smirks, his face is as narrow as a jar. He is a seedy kitchen rake drawn by Edward Lear.

Each of us has coveted the two eggs that have furnished the egg basket since this afternoon, but these will be reserved for the undernourished children till more are laid. Butter, every last lick, is gone. There is wheat and cooking oil, but not much more. We are approaching one of those frequent all-time lows. Only the two stunted tamarillo trees are stooped in abundance.

No one knows what Bruce is conjuring. Those patrolling the range, as you do in times of hunger, have observed the muslin bag of milk curds hung, dripping, on the butcher's hook over the sourdough bug to turn to cottage cheese overnight. In the afternoon hours, we have heard Bruce turning the grinder bicycle wheels. He is Delphic in his preparations, non-revelatory. Total absorption, his.

We salivate. All except my father. In his eyes Bruce's tart is the fruit of pure narcissism: one-off performance cookery inspired by munchies. The antipathy is mutual. Bruce dubs my father an *old woman*—we women are alive to the misogyny of this—and so divides Manaroa along political lines. There are those who understand my father's commitment to the hard graft of sourcing three square vegetarian meals a day. And there are those, mostly heavy marijuana users, mostly male, who see in my father's insistence on nutrition an infringement of their right to anarchy and chaos.

Around midnight the concave Scot delivers. His *Tamarillo Brillo* is the stuff of instant legend; he coins the name on the spot. A sweet–sour tart made from sourdough crust filled with honeyed custard and tamarillo, this a dish of exquisite delicacy, and it comes direct from the imagination of Bruce.

Cultivator of solitudinous diary-hours and early nights, my father has long gone up to the Island and his packing-case sleepout. I stash him a slice of Tamarillo Brillo in the storeroom safe. *Stashing*: a practice explicitly frowned on but routinely practised. Kate stashes another slice for my sister. Kim's slice of Tamarillo Brillo glides into the sunroom on a sturdy white New Zealand Railways china saucer, clasped between the tattooed thumb and forefinger of her mother, Dean.

Handles

Who this defiantly working-class man is, no one knows. One day, Hooki simply drives up in an indigo van with his black mongrel, Jimbo. Manaroa is so discouragingly deep in the Marlborough Sounds, three or four hours by largely unsealed road, that you don't stumble upon our commune but have to set your mind to it. In Hooki's case, having arrived and knowing no one, man and dog persist.

Hooki is a carpenter and self-taught blacksmith, and these trades, plus a memorable traffic in deadpan, ensure him a peripheral place at Manaroa. Literally, for the newcomer takes up residence just beyond the back gate of the kitchen garden, unrolling his swag in the mezzanine of the steeple-topped woodshed under the pine belt. From there he sets about making himself useful.

I note the flinty contour of his forehead and chin, as if he were made from one of his trade's extra-durable materials. And after a certain amount of strenuously low-key interaction at hob and wood block, I discover Hooki to be a Londoner of impressive comic timing, adamantine melancholy and simmering paranoia.

My delicate cultivation of Hooki must be working because, one day, he offers to forge a handle for my caravan door. I lack one of those. The result of his impromptu smithying is an impressively medieval thing that is an ill fit for my caravan's shoddy aluminium door and plunges blackly into the grass at my feet every few twists. The dungeonesque handle gives me a kick, in both senses, every time I turn it.

In the bracken

It has been a year since I lived with Katie Vinke and her family in the A-frame with daffodils, but it feels longer. Deep in relationship with strawberry-blond Tom, Katie probably feels the same. What I can say is that when she and Tom disembark at Manaroa pier, her dubiousness about visiting is apparent. That's Katie and me: an uneasy coalition. Forever wrong-footed by the idea that we should be friends, we are, in practice, incompatible. I throw myself into the role of host with gusto.

At my initiative, we muck around performing self-consciously Manaroan things. Visiting the Land. Lighting the range for tea. Going topless in the sun. Passing the toke along the sofa in the conversationally sparse after-dinner kitchen circle. None of which Katie takes to. She doesn't even like the soiled vintage dress-ups, provided by our community chest, with which I woo her. Instead, Katie sticks close to the girlfriend–boyfriend unit, and I observe Tom itching to step further, deeper, into this new world. It is apparent he is considering me anew. I don't care a jot for this boy of the painfully sharp angles, but it is vindicating to command the attention of the one who shunned me on our single Hitching Post date.

As it is summer, and we have a full house, Manaroa turns out the full commune cliché for my visitors, capped by firelight under the stars with accompanying guitars. I am almost able to fulfil my role in this theatre of the easy-going. Through a veil of shooting sparks, however, I am aware of Tom and Katie arguing under their breath. They've been fretting at each other like this all day. Now, Katie prevails, and Tom follows her reluctantly to bed.

When I come in later, Katie is pressed up against the caravan wall, asleep. Tom is rolled against her. There is nowhere else for the guests to sleep but my double bed. I join them, creeping under the covers and positioning myself on the bed's very edge. It is one thing to play cool by day, another to relax in a shared bed. When Tom's hand reaches out for me, I don't resist—this doesn't occur to my quick-fire body. Then we're kissing.

Only a short time passes, but when Katie erupts from the bed Tom and I have almost forgotten her. In the angry scramble she makes across our bodies, we are recalled. Katie stands spitting in the middle of the small space. Then she's gone.

Swinging his feet over the side of the bed, Tom makes no move to follow. Rather, he simply remains, head lowered, sharp blond curtains of hair twitching in irritation. It strikes me that this is what Tom is: an irritable old man. More, right now he is extraneous, and he seems to know it.

I rush off, out the door, after Katie. Follow her down the stubbly pasture towards the creek, running to catch up. Right before the creek, Katie trips, stumbles and falls into a heap of bracken and fern. I join her there.

Once we are down, there is nowhere left to go and not much to do, either. It is springy as a harsh nest, the bracken. After a period of struggle and détente, I am able to inch an arm around Katie's waist. In the short prickly history of our friendship, this is closer, in a completely fucked-up way, than I have gotten or will ever get again to Katie. We don't speak. Katie sobs, then dozes. I lie awake in the state of calm that is mine after I have experienced or done an awful thing.

This memory is a splinter that has taken up permanent residence under my skin. The peevish string of betrayals: Katie's getting together with Tom, followed by my transgression. Strangest is my reverse-loyalty to Katie and the way it turns so desperately on a dime. You could read a tale of vengeance in my night moves with her and Tom.

Closer to the mark, I am seventeen. Competitiveness, vanity, insecurity and fecklessness vie with touch-paper sexuality and a need to please. My amorality is as mobile as my sympathy.

Festival of rain

The rainfall here is legendary. Perhaps we are entering Macondo—city of mirrors and mirages, also founded on a river plain—where it rained for four years, eleven months and two days. Only this is the West Coast of the South Island, New Zealand, where it also rains and rains but somewhat less famously.

A dog-eared paperback of Gabriel García Márquez's *One Hundred Years of Solitude* has recently passed from hand to hand like a fever dream at the Pines. The queue to read has been as long and contagious as the winter rain that silver-papers our windows. Now, the novel's hallucinatory suggestiveness colours my journey by mailboat out of Pelorus Sound. I am going to Punakaiki Festival.

In Nelson, I meet an Englishman, filling his house truck with festivalgoers, who offers me a seat upfront in the cab. Just before the tiny West Coast town of Punakaiki, we turn inland through a landscape so richly unfamiliar, so manifestly ancient that I almost check for a sauropod plunging out of the rainforest. Eventually, we join a procession of vehicles approaching farm gates, beyond which a riverside paddock is tilled by tepees, tarps, motorbikes, house trucks and converted buses. There are women in anklets with Pre-Raphaelite hair, and men with radiant bare torsos. There's even a goat or two that some resourceful back-to-the-lander has brought along to milk for the three-day duration.

With the festival entertainments spread out in an extemporised feast, I mill, observe, sample. Nudity and toplessness, in which I participate, go unremarked. Tents and marquees provide access to massage, meditation and chanting sessions; to juggling, craft, four-part harmony and a rumoured levitation workshop. Dancing to live bands at one of several stages takes much of my time, but I keep an eye out for postings for the levitation workshop. My scepticism is rewarded when it is serially postponed.

On the first night at dusk a Tolkien obsessive floats candles on rafts improvised from giant leaves down the Nile River. If not a Macondo, there is at least a Nile. I know Robin as the erudite and bespectacled man who built a retreat, with a hand-shingled pagoda roof, high in the bush-clad hills behind the Pines, largely solo. This was the Fairy Cottage, a project too ambitiously conceived and remote to ever be completed with available resources.

I once hiked up to the Fairy Cottage to spend a single night on my own and test a nerve I did not possess. Electing in the spirit of the thing to fast, I arrived with my novel and candlestick and found absolutely nothing to do in the single room that opened onto a balcony with missing slats and a view over the Sound. Half ruin already, open at unglazed windows and unhung door, the Fairy Cottage belonged to marsupials and moonlight. Sleep would not come. A pair of possums played chase along the balcony—a quick, noisy circumference of the cottage and back again—bitching all the way.

I woke to an unfamiliar pressure on my chest, two gloaming eyes on mine. A possum crouched there. I leapt first. Then possum, who shot out an unglazed window. At first light, I followed. Back down the hill to the Pines.

After a fitful sleep in the cab of the Punakaiki house truck, I climb into the back and find myself sardined between the driver and other strangers. In between wandering hands (his), the talkative Englishman tells me he earned his crust as a magician in London. *You remind me of Kate Bush,* he finishes up. By this I understand him to mean that because he once had sex with Kate Bush in London, I will have sex with him in Punakaiki. I consider his connections but not his offer. I adore 'Wuthering Heights' but have been raised to scorn all name-droppers.

Of more interest is a woman in a leather jacket who is weaving the festival fringes on the back of a motorcycle, a woman always on her way somewhere else, with inky hair, delicate profile and unusually solid shoes. Stamped on my peripheral vision, she appears frail but queenly. I stash the vision for later.

Nailed to a time and a marquee, the levitation workshop proves disappointingly earthbound. Based on a conceptual *as if,* not one of our lotus positions lifts off the canvas. We are too unevolved, too distant from enlightenment to levitate, is the word on the street.

On this third and last morning—the morning we learn levitation is not for the likes of us; the morning the festival is de-populating and the accumulated human squalor apparent; the morning on which, with less to do and ever less inclination to do it, anything might happen—into this exhausted mood walks Raoul. Drawn together by a disenchantment we don't yet admit, we set off along the forest trails.

In a river clearing fringed by toe toe, our strangers' talk gives out and, as if on cue, we begin to feel each other up. Even more awkward than usual, our fumbles are laughably half-hearted. Standing on the big river stones, we drop our hands to our sides. I don't know who goes first. I've never heard a boy talk like this: of clumsy seduction, dutiful gropes, bad faith and lack of feeling. These brief, broken histories are mine too and I reciprocate in kind. We wish to put an end to pretending.

I see Raoul on my way back to Manaroa via Nelson. He is light in forgetful clothes. It would be unfair not to mention the blue eyes. I cross a grass tennis court with him and an acquaintance from Nelson Girls'. As we walk, I wonder if there is anything left to talk about with this intimate stranger. And, so it is. After the acquaintance splits off, and we go for grape juice at the Hitching Post, Raoul disappears in one or other of the tidal shifts that continually sweep the hippy movement and I never see him again.

Chanel No. 5

I visit my father's house on the Island and there she is. My eye falls on the pair of crutches laid neatly on the floor and then on their owner again in her battered biker jacket, jeans and native beauty spot, her damask camisole and orthopaedic shoes. Doused in Chanel No. 5, a scent competing with rumours of an unemptied chamber pot, Janine perches, exquisite in shades of noir, on the edge of my father's princess-and-the-pea arrangement of kapok mattresses. There is nowhere else for those making a social call, or engaging in one of my father's hand readings, to sit.

My father is propped against the north wall, fully dressed under a blanket or two, and wearing a beanie as is his custom when in bed filling his diary with longhand. I plop down right where you fetch up on opening the door—south end of the mattress stack. And there we are: three awkward points in an unfamiliar social geometry that forms, quite literally, a triangle.

After I have made it my business to out my father's possible pisspot, the traveller makes it hers to befriend the rude, curious girl I am. A botany student of Māori–French descent, Janine is a handful of years and a world of experience older than me. In years to come, we will be nocturnal flâneurs of the Wellington streets, our pace set by the swinging throw of her crutches. Don't imagine these last an impediment to splendour. The crutches are ballast to the piratic beauty-shock of their mistress-ship, the black sails of her hair. Together we will eyeball obscure bass players in smoky rooms, trade satirical notes in op-shop lurex and relish the slow night music that is our progress home down Cuba, along Dixon and up Courtenay Place in the scrappy capital's deserted hours.

Right now, however, arriving at this improvisory house in this improvisory afternoon hour, I am concerned to establish that neither my father nor Janine has made an unlikely conquest of the other. He wouldn't make a pass, would he? My father is quick to strike a verbal rapport, the room is pretty much a bed, and this attractive newcomer is barely older than

me. My pre-emptive pisspot strike is a double-pronged attack not-so-subliminally intended to lower his sexual status and express my disgust at the very thought. Maintaining a modest airiness and an elusive eyeline, my father dodges the subtext. I need not worry. In time I will discover that Janine's tastes run to the kind of young male beauty that, in his late thirties, my father patently is not.

Even so, my insensitive appearance disturbs whatever fragile ecology is struggling to establish itself between these strangers. After a further trickle of small talk, I disembark my father's shipwrecked barque and head down to the main house where, I am pleased to note, Janine appears soon after.

Hash cookies

Like everything Bruce occasionally cooks, the hash cookies are superb. I blithely eat three. Later, I find out that hardened users limit themselves to one. Later is two days away when Bruce, feeling mildly responsible but mostly just keen to dispense advice, visits my bedside. My physical tremors and identity shakes have not yet subsided.

I first notice all is not right when I leave the kitchen gloom and daylight assaults me in frames. Instead of the integrated and continuously unfolding optical image I take for granted, the garden path is a series of jump cuts. Of randomly looming and receding perspectives whose connecting frames are missing.

There is loss of balance, sweating and dry retching. Worst is the internal revolt. Encountering my father doesn't help. His panicked line of questioning comes at me like the foliage. Outsize and out of sympathy. A teetotaller is the last person you need in a drug- or alcohol-related situation.

Another's enfolding arm guides me back to the house. I float up to the ceiling and look down at myself. *Am I dying or dead already? How do I get back?* Someone guides me to bed in the front room. Dean perhaps, but I cannot be sure. I am being dunked in a dark sea.

Later, Sylvie brings herbal tea and sits with me. Later still, I am the object of unusual solicitude from the hardcore users. Rob advises that even he ate only two cookies and these over a number of hours. Bruce smiles his snaggletooth sneer and opines that his solution would have been to eat another cookie. After a day or two I can face my father, who sits by the bed in uncomprehending fury. He hates drugs in any form, believing them uncouth. In his books, their rewiring of perception is as good as unholy. Now he sits by the bedside as green as I and even more afraid. I cold-shoulder him. On the third day, psychological parts shakily reassembled, I get up.

Sudden views

Late one night after inhaling a few puffs, I witness Paul shuffle into the Pines's smoky kitchen wearing his dark wool coat and hair-trigger smile. I don't think I've ever seen this sweet-natured and peripatetic man out of either. Apparently invisible to everyone else is the smouldering shape attached to Paul's chest by four sets of claws. From my position on the couch, I see a featureless mass without a face, a marsupial the colour and substance of smoke, riding our visitor. A psychic parasite draining Paul at core. I am stoned. These insights occur in flashes.

I close my eyes and sob. When I look again, Paul sits in the club chair by the door, hair falling across his face, no sign of the beast. I think about telling him what I have seen but it is too disturbing.

There is a beast of similar description in Ursula Le Guin's *The Wizard of Earthsea*, a book I read once as a child, and then every year after. The creature that visits Ged is the size of a young child and headless, a black beast with four taloned paws unleashed during an overly flashy demonstration of the wizard's powers. Have I witnessed Paul's shadow-self, seeking form? A harrowing possibility, and one I have no idea what to do with.

A few weeks later, Paul is sectioned by a Nelson psychiatric unit after climbing the fence *to sniff the naked ladies* growing inside a stranger's front garden. His humorous reference to the scented pink lily *Amaryllis belladonna* is lost on the homeowner. Paul has two brothers: Steve, the younger and spunkier; and my favourite, Marty, who has the witty physique of a spider monkey and is as clever as a doctor. The Nelson tidings reach us at Manaroa via one or other of these brothers, transforming Paul into a folk hero.

Mental illness is rarely named in the hippy world, where a capacious but vague tolerance rules. The rejection of medical labels is idealistic, as if illness might be rethought or outstepped by dispensing with the official language. Sometimes, however, it feels as if no one wants to be bothered by the specifics.

In Paul's case, his two devoted brothers visit the psych unit where he is held and, in relatively short time, he is released back into the community.

After the hash cookie and the astral possum, it is clear that, if Paul is dogged by certain frailties or susceptibilities, I am too. In future I will pass the joint without inhaling. I won't miss the pungent sweetness or the havoc it wrecks with my brain.

As for the bamboo bong—whose stink-water has permanently watermarked the velveteen couch and probably, if you look closer, Bruce himself—it has never tempted.

One day, however, a hessian sack of cactus arrives by mail boat. Is it the Thompson twins who have lopped off the head of a prized suburban specimen and sliced it into weeping cross sections? The famous green slime to which these are reduced in an outdoor cauldron in the Manaroa garden *is* memorable. We stand around joking and pulling faces as it simmers over a morning. The reputation of cactus for a pantheistic vibe and for puking precedes it. Eventually someone—Bruce, maybe—decants the pale green gloop into Vegemite jars and mugs. Weighing the merits, controlling the gag reflex, I slither my half jar down. After that there is nothing to do but go on a collective afternoon jaunt to the coastal foothills, minus my non-imbibing father and the children.

Low-wattage beatitude among pebbles, pasture and sky ensues. Busy communing with nature and my fellow stoners, I still have time to register that it is all a bit inane. Like a phony family outing with sudden views of plants. Most disorienting of all is seeing Bruce out under the levelling sky, liberated from sofa-reign and derogatory commentary. That is something.

Rather than anything visionary, it is the suspension of group politics and bitchy takedowns that makes the day memorable. Maybe we spend too much time inside. Maybe we just need to get out more.

Portals

With so many hours to dispose of I immerse myself in calculating the position of the planets and their spokes of relation.

Astrology: Sylvie inducts me into the maths and consultation of the *American Ephemeris*, counting forward from Greenwich Mean Time (GMT) for Southern Hemisphere hours and locations. Calculations complete, I am able to plot a person's natal chart on a pad of templates Sylvie loans me.

Years on, when I am living in Wellington, I bump into a journalist who tells me I once spent a couple of hours interpreting his astrological chart in person. I am impressed that my nineteen-year-old self found so much to impart to this man in corduroy pants, worn black Oxfords and op-shop shirt, asthmatic laugh and inhaler. But then, Tom Scully—baroquely courteous artist of the self-undoing sentence-loop, spinner and rescinder of endless possibility—would have been the perfect respondent.

Browsing the interpretative volumes between the caravan bookshelves and sunroom library at the Pines, I find the commentaries can be hard to swallow; are often harsh and fatalistic in a way that conspires with my self-hating teen-extremism.

The astrological placing of Neptune conjunct Mars in Scorpio in the Eighth House signifies that its natives are susceptible to occult possession, I read. Tell that to a seventeen-year-old and watch her imagination inflame. I have this placing. I also have a T-square, like Napoleon. Of this I learn that internal oppositions and tensions of character, and the illusion of something missing in their make-up, engender suffering in the native but may also drive them to achieve great things. I feel depressed just reading this—already fulfilling the prophesy. Actually, in my case the aspect is wide, just outside the seven-degree zone of qualification, and therefore equivocal. I hover in a limbo of uneasy identification.

My chart also has what is known as the bowl configuration of planets—in my case, inverted. This, I read, means things will forever be upending in the native's life: possessions, situations, relationships. *Bummer*, as B. Ware would say. I wonder if the inverted bowl is the *just passing through* hippy trope reconfigured, the *travel light* mantra. I find no evidence for this, but nothing to refute it, either. Hungry for self-knowledge, I gulp down more astrological punishment.

I take the Neptune–Mars conjunction and its warning about occult possession to heart and worry about ghosts and other malevolent entities. Behind the kitchen garden and along the pine belt, darkness drapes into hostile folds. Crossing these territories on the way to bed, we have only our lanterns or the moon to ruffle night's black nap. The nightmares that roughed childhood's counterpane, deranging my life in the year before I left my parents', return as occult narratives. Sometimes I feel as if the night might simply catch fire. By day I know better than to speak of this for fear of inviting the unseen in. I am alone in psychic flammability.

Eventually I do speak of it. To Sylvie as we sit in a circle of outdoor firelight. It is summer; we have visitors—ergo the fire. *You can close the portal*, she advises. *Speak your intention and the visits will cease.*

Say it out loud?

Say it inside your mind. Address whatever you see or sense and tell it you're not ready. Sylvie's mouth sets in a comfortingly stubborn line. *Say that you don't want any more visits, thank you.* She crosses her arms and stares mildly into the flames. Her solution is so sensible: a simple, earthly kind of magic within my reach.

Back at my caravan, I follow her instruction to the letter. I clarify my wish to be left alone. I hold this intention in my mind, much as you do when you are asking the *I Ching* a question. Then I forget about it. True to Sylvie's promise, the nightmares of possession stop. The bewitched unknown beyond the firelight goes quiet. My wish is upheld.

But portals are evanescent places. Tidal. The waves come in and out and return over the years. An especially malevolent ghoul assails me in a dream set in an underground car park, over a decade after the Manaroa silencing. My assailant from the other side approaches menacingly, dripping with ectoplasm like a fright-creature from a horror film. I stand there, locked in, unable to run or retreat or lift a finger to save myself. Suddenly, right before the ghoul strikes, I pipe up: *Thank you*. Something flows into me. Grace. I can feel the ghoul feel it too. *Thank you.* I really mean it. And, just like that, the ghoul cedes power and desire to harm me. In dream, I watch it fade away.

Eventually my love affair with astrology begins to feel one-sided. If I like astrology it doesn't always like me. Its cosmic geometries fuel doubt. Just starting out in adult life, I want an open field unconstrained by second- or third-hand readings of my character. I have become conscious of the way that astrology's declarations render me passive. My father's dreams and portents often seem to have this effect on him. I think of him brooding on a blond woman, sighted on the Cook Strait ferry, whom he never meets but remains certain is his soul mate. For years no other woman can approach this presentiment. While dreaming of a projected future, the present is slipping away. I ditch astrology on my own behalf but continue in the divination of others. I am kinder and more optimistic when it comes to others.

I had a dream

My father enjoys the discussions of karma, past lives, soul mates and other issues of spiritual evolution that pepper hippy discourse. Vague, speculative and magic realist as they are, these ruminations and assertions are like good stories. Occasionally I throw in the odd curly question about historical atrocities and genocide, to which I never receive a satisfactory answer. Otherwise, I keep my mind and ears open.

The concept of a behavioural balance sheet is familiar. I was introduced to something similar in Bible class at otherwise-secular Kelburn Normal primary school. Nothing in my atheist upbringing had prepared me for Canon Joblin's weekly visit, which appeared as abruptly as it was later removed from the syllabus. Playing up in his first afternoon class, I wrote a crudely illustrated note: *What does Canon Joblin fire out of his canon?*

My indignation at this imperious man and his doctrine was embodied in this not-quite-rhetorical question passed, hand to hand, under the desks. In an orgy of primary school wit, my classmates responded with *jobbies*, *poo* and *wee*. The cannon I had drawn resembled a penis aimed at three o'clock and we had our bodily functions scrambled but the note was a runaway success. That is until Canon Joblin intercepted it.

After that a different kind of note accompanied me home. My grandmother responded to this report of my bad behaviour by having me pen the homily *Treat others as you would have them treat you* in fancy floral script. I did so with only a little ill grace because, in fact, I agreed with both the principle and the method of her lesson. When I was done, my grandmother pinned this felt-pen equivalent of an embroidered sampler to our living-room wall.

*

My parents' belief that they won't be taking another turn on the karmic wheel of death and rebirth is more of a turn-off. Estranged, they share a sense of spiritual high status—too highly evolved to come back for another round of reincarnation—but only in relation to themselves not each other. I quiz my father again—*What do you mean you won't be coming back for another round on the wheel?*—for the pleasure of hearing him indict himself further. It is not the wheel that bothers me—the wheel being the grandly intricate, karmic wheel of life and rebirth that, thanks to Tibetan Buddhism, enjoys currency in hippy conversation. No, it is the temerity of thinking you might be done with its revolutions.

My sister and I know that our father is susceptible to auto suggestion. His dreams fall under the same rubric. These range from *I had a dream I need to get more vitamin B* to *I had a dream you could murder your mother if you don't get your feelings about her sorted*. The latter is addressed to me after an unhappy visit up the valley to the house where she lives with Heinz.

Why would you need to dream about vitamin B intake when you can read about it in one of those boring health books, and probably just have? Matricide gives me more pause. *Don't worry, we've all been murderers in past lives*, my father sighs. That is his version of comfort. Intelligent as he is, valiantly unconventional, there are days when he clips the lunatic fringe. I decide that he must be talking about his own feelings, even if he doesn't realise it. I am familiar with the concept of projection. And yet, something of his egalitarian attitude regarding our dark capabilities and culpabilities remains. It is a salutary thought that we might all make murderers—an insight that history tends to back up. That thought sneaks through the barrier of teenage scepticism and takes permanent root in my imagination, in my peripheral understanding of who we might be.

Years later, when I am at design school in Wellington, my father phones to continue the riff. *I had a dream you could give birth to your reincarnated Uncle Martin.*

I hold the receiver of the phone closer to my ear. *Martin? But he's dead.*

My father is unmoved. He has his oracle voice on. *Reincarnated Martin. I think he might choose you to be reborn to.*

I realise there is gallantry at work here, and just for a flash I do feel weirdly flattered. It seems to be a compliment that Martin might select me as future mother and birth canal. Perhaps this is another gesture of comfort? Martin is coming back. These delusions notwithstanding, I think the idea in really bad taste. Even so, I have a vision of Martin with self-cut pudding basin hair and Nehru-collared shirt emerging fully formed, feet first, from a vagina. *My* vagina. No way.

When I still lived with him, Martin cut the collars off his shirts and hand-stitched the edges closed, some with statement flowery bias binding. His half-sister, my renegade mother, figured in his inspirations. Despite my grandmother's censure of her, he knew that my mother's sartorial daring stood for both itself and something else: another way of seeing. He was fashioning himself in subtle ways that spoke to his convictions.

But now he is freshly dead by his own hand and, although I grieve him, I do not believe him coming back. Not ever.

Unable to banish the thought of his rebirth, I tell my mother, who is on a rare visit to Wellington for Art Business. She is sitting in the kitchen in my flatmate Fay's white vinyl hairdresser's chair—a salvaged item that still sports its heating hood. My mother's current art dealer sits across the table. I recount my father's vision because I don't know where else to put it. Perhaps I am searching for approval by way of showing off. Reliably, my mother escalates the imagery by adding a shoe-shine brush. A creature of constant industry herself, this is just what she sees: Martin, mid-rebirth, shining his shoes. Nor does she forget his rhyming, shining, button eyes. She loved her half-brother; is no stranger to the outlandish. We dissolve into hysterics. After that, I try not to think of my father's prediction ever again.

After Muybridge

At primary school, if you can draw a horse—in particular, a horse in motion—it is settled. You can draw. This is one way to navigate the fickle complexities of classroom popularity. One of my first school drawings is a skin-coloured horse, looking more like a bull, with tremendous shoulders and wide gait. In him, I partake of the post-Muybridge rite of passage for the child artist: the unsupported transit of horse legs, all four in the air at once. Perched at the base of this bulky hybrid's upraised wing, a hastily drawn female emoticon, with the white–blond hair I recently owned, grins.

I'm not sure where the drawing gets me in the classroom hierarchies, but my Pegasus does communicate ecstatic ambition around the possibilities of speed and representation. Just above the horse's mohawk, the words *Good bye* sail by in cursive. She's going places, this infant artist and her avatar in pigtails—*fast.*

Ever since I can remember I have been drawing Biro

portraits, featuring heavily flowered gowns and hypnotically circled eyes, on whatever is to hand. An opened-out Benson & Hedges cigarette packet, a brown paper bag. My mother lined the walls with those drawings. She had just started making her own art—oil paintings and clay icons—but valued mine as highly. You would be forgiven for thinking I drew to capture my mother's elusive approval. I did capture it, but drawing was its own reward. While I was concentrating on making Biro lines on the page or thick fields of oil pastel colour, something opened between us.

She taught me how to blow eggs for egg dolls, pricking the end with a needle and blowing out reluctant streamers of yolk and white. I painted the hollow shells with elliptical faces and crowned them with serrated foil. Only queens, no kings. Gorgeously frangible portraits of my mother and myself at one remove. They never lasted. One flick of a breeze or passing sleeve and they were dashed. My mother would harp on the loss until I made another. She worshipped those egg dolls.

Now the hours hang sufficiently heavy at the Pines to reawaken my appetite for mimesis. I write a letter to the School Publications Branch in Wellington. It seems amazing that this national institution agrees to see a seventeen-year-old school-leaver, but they do. A senior editor replies to my letter. They would be happy to take a look at my work if I would like to ring to arrange a time. Not long after, I take the voyage out of the Sounds.

Packed with commissioned poetry, fiction, non-fiction and illustration, the School Journals have been a reference for New Zealand children since the early twentieth century. My father's occasional freelance writing for the journal ensures me a contact at head office. My mother once wrote children's fiction for School Pubs too, but I don't know this at the time. It is Robyn Belton, the Nelson illustrator and my art teacher's wife, whose example is on my mind.

At School Pubs, the senior editor invites another commissioning editor to view my sixth-form art portfolio. Conscious of appreciative murmurings in the kindly New Zealand way, and of women who wear their expertise lightly, I muster sudden verbal fluency. Something works, for I leave the offices elated, trial commission in hand.

The porter

Travelling home from the interview I am a little too in love with the possibilities that life is so obligingly unfolding. In this mood, sneaking up onto a cordoned-off upper deck of the Cook Strait ferry, for a solitary box-seat view of Wellington's hill-ringed harbour, is irresistible.

Here, the porter finds me. A smile-creased older man, English, he rests on the railing, asking me this and that. I think his conversation disarmingly existential for a man in uniform. The uniform counts: it leads me to underestimate him. After a while, the porter confesses that he is not allowed to converse with passengers above decks. Not only will I be in trouble for straying onto an off-limits area, but he will be too if caught fraternising. He's nice, so I follow him. Down one deck, then another. Through a stiff-hinged *Crew Only* door. Along a narrow white metal corridor. It's labyrinthine in the guts of the ship. Where are we going?

I feel slightly foolish in my cotton dress of clashing pink and black geometry, another skirt underneath, my beret. It seemed so right when I selected it for School Pubs. Now it is *noisy.* Have you ever noticed that wearing the wrong clothes can lead to wrong actions? It is as if one becomes subtly unfamiliar to oneself. I compensate for this off-centre feeling by following the porter into the ship innards. The industrial clatter and stench of galley food, the clatter and shout of unseen men going about their business, touch me with the chill possibility of being seen, here, in the company of this or any man. In argument with self-preserving instinct, empathy wins. I keep going, riding a one-way current of passivity in the porter's wake.

I am well acquainted with meaning-of-life nerds trapped in men's bodies. I don't give a toss for the meaning of life but, in this case, it is a blessing that the porter is an autodidact philosopher. It keeps him busy. His quarters are Spartan. Narrow bed, porthole of waves, hard chair. I manage an unnaturally bright performance in the question-and-answer dance. Porter leading; me parrying. Porter on the chair; me standing.

When he draws me in to hold my waist and touch my face, I stiffen with aversion. Standing outside myself, a relationship that makes me slow to act, I am aware of the porter's loneliness. Of his opportunism and middle age. Of my own repulsion. I maintain decoy chatter, preserving him from rejection. But the porter is no fool. Abruptly, he seems to tire of maintaining the charade of mutuality and retires his hands.

Hurrying back down the ship's high-gloss intestines towards daylight, it hits me with sickening clarity how recklessly I entered this foreign geography, how far I came not knowing the way back.

In print

In the sanctuary of my own high-gloss metal cell I consider my commission, an illustrated border for a verse about kitchen mice running amok.

I take a trip to the Pines kitchen to make preliminary sketches of kitchen utensils, macaroni and pulses in Agee jars and other props. I scour the sunroom shelves for rodent references. Beatrix Potter sets the standard. Propped against my caravan wall, I replenish my Rotring pen and ink up a surround of pointillist mice cavorting on pantry shelves, and then another and another until I am satisfied.

In due course I receive my first ever *With Compliments* slip and two copies of the journal with cover artwork by Robyn Belton. When I crack the spine my duotone border produces equal parts fretfulness and pleasure. Is the draughtsmanship timid? The answer to this is embodied in a cheque in a franked envelope and a further commission. Just shy of eighteen *and a jobbing illustrator*. Almost. I savour everything about the print world: art supplies, page constraints and—best and worst—the printed object in my hand.

The next children's poem features a pig in a shawl en route to a moonlit assignation. Four-colour this time, instead of two; I have risen in the hierarchy of print. The possibilities of chiaroscuro, drapery and the pig's palpable sense of mission are as seductive as the technical specs and materials. I wet and stretch the watercolour paper, adhering it to a board with brown butcher's tape. As it is routine for a sheet to buckle, I prepare two like this. Then I wait for the paper to dry before ruling trim marks for the printer to the dimensions of the finished artwork. These stages are precisely observed before I can even begin to think about applying paint. Thick Arches watercolour paper, tubes of acrylic, wide-gauge butcher's tape and the two sable brushes I bought with my own money for sixth-form art.

Life studies follow. For these I hike off to the Land armed with a bucket of kitchen scraps and a sketch pad to observe Miss Piggly and the litter she has produced with her grown son. As the pigs rootle and bicker among the potato peelings, I rehearse their swoop of contour and resistance of muscle. Down at mud level it is possible to tune in to the ineffable pigness of pigs. No one tells you they are beautiful.

In the ballroom my sister consents to hunker on all fours, crochet shawl tied about her shoulders, so that I can observe the drapery sculpt. We have moments of affinity and complicity that cohere around imaginative projects, but fail to bloom into friendship. Does the energy consumed by the atomised relations with our mother, the severances and repairs and rivalry, consume our emotional stamina for each other? Or is it that we have only ever spent a few months living together? Either way, compatibility is a luxury that family conditions haven't given us time to test. Briefly, we enjoy creative collaboration in the Pines ballroom.

The pine-tree belt behind the kitchen garden inspires a silhouette for the protagonist pig to trot past. My early, post-Muybridge Pegasus turns out to have been a trial run. This time the challenge is trotters churning air. Woody greens, flesh pinks, Arabian-night blue: I keep the palette deep and soft. A hush radiates from the centre of the completed artwork where the shawl-draped pig passes in pink secrecy under dusky pines and lantern moon.

When it appears in print, I find someone at School Publications has widened the pig's eye in black felt-tip pen. The clumsy emphasis rankles; I try not to let this splinter of dissatisfaction spoil the picture.

John of Saratoga and Jane

I do not wish for John of Saratoga to sink below the horizon unremarked. The act of remembering him, however, must square up to another's attempt to obliterate him. Less than three years after I first meet him, John of Saratoga is murdered in a railway sleeper carriage where he lies in the arms of his lover.

He is murdered by Jane's estranged husband and, in the same bloody breath, so is she.

Just like that this character of ramshackle resilience ceases to exist, and so does she: their deaths are more agonising than *just like* and *so does* can suggest.

The news comes by mail boat via a visitor, who tells us, additionally, of the perpetrator's failed suicide by ritual disembowelling. Jane's ex, Warren, had been reading Yukio Mishima, mining the details of the author's obsession with the samurai practice of seppuku. Now he has multiplied the obscenity of Mishima's own famously botched suicide, a decade previously, with double murder. Warren has beheaded John and then Jane by sword. It is impossible not to note the grotesque pretension of the thing.

I learn of these impossible deaths at the Pines gate, which opens inward to our kitchen garden or outward onto the valley that rolls down to the Sound and the incoming tidings.

Far from telephones and electricity, from newspapers or courts of law, our friends' murder clouds the glass of our sheltered lives. In the absence of anything to be done, we don't know how to do it. Kate and Rob journey to the funeral and wake; the rest of us lie low. We are unused to truck with the world of officialdom even where it might concern us. My father says he once stood by Warren in the Pines garden, and that he bristled with the most violence he had ever encountered in another human being. For once, I am not sceptical of his intuition.

The murder trial verdict reduces the magnitude of the deed in the historical record by judging it a crime of passion and downgrading the sentence to the lesser charge of manslaughter. There is contesting evidence. Warren arranged for his and Jane's two young children to travel to Christchurch before he committed the murders some distance away in Kaikōura. He got the children out of the way, in other words. Kate, who had been with John of Saratoga the day of his death and with Warren the same evening, travels to the Blenheim courtroom to testify to the latter's premeditation of the double-murder. At Manaroa, we read the court's sentence as a grave miscarriage of justice.

I have only recently seen John of Saratoga with his new love, in what are, unbeknownst, the last months of his life. He's coming in the same Pines garden gate as news of his death will later travel. He is as crookedly handsome as ever, hair drawn back to expose a high forehead and one tenderly outsize ear. It is impossible to miss the fact that John has come out in love: a shy man, of gallows humour, happily exposing himself to the strong New Zealand light.

Later, I pass him in the paddock on my side of the creek, sitting on a log by the remnants of an open fire. He is rubbing a rollie between blackened nails, alternately giggling and coughing. An unfamiliar woman shares the log, as rail-thin as he. Jane has a raunchier laugh than John. You can tell she leads the merriment, has called forth John of Saratoga's pluck. They are like a pair of old children, John and Jane, twinned in mutual bedazzlement.

That love has found John of Saratoga, a man routinely

impoverished in self-care, is much commented on at the time. We have seen the evidence. And that is how we remember him. A man in love, newly chatty, right to the stop of his death.

A hole in time

A second thing happens on the day that news of John of Saratoga's murder reaches Manaroa. When everyone has downed tools to sit as if turned to stone or wander in circles, when the hours themselves are sickly, Doug drops anchor at the bay in the finery of someone else's speedboat. Charged with delivering this large vessel elsewhere in the Sounds, Doug has detoured to take us for a ride. He has not heard the news.

Even when he has, the only thing that remains is to clamber over the polished rails and aboard. Sylvie conjures a loaf of sourdough and a pot of honey. It is summer and we are going boating in the most dreadful, the most hallucinated, of circumstances. Even Rob decides to come.

We coast, steering clear of the unpredictable waters of the open Sound, hugging the sheltered coves. In a deserted inlet, we drop anchor and dispose ourselves on the boat's unfamiliar surfaces. Unacquainted with maritime leisure, with idling on decks, we embrace this hole in time.

There's Kate, bare-breasted with long, scrub-chipped limbs.

Then Rob exposing his peppery-white body to the crystal light.

B. Ware gets naked without ceremony. Gentled by atrocity, she is mild today. I notice, as I sometimes do, that her large hazel eyes harbour secret lights.

I dive off the rails, deliberately splashing Doug. He laughs a suggestible laugh, encouraging me to splash him further. We splash the delirium of the day back and forth. From a cool spot on the deck, I wonder at the way we lurch from grief to joy and back again.

Back at Manaroa, I pass Doug as he is coming into the kitchen and I am leaving for the night. We fumble in and out of each other's arms. Then I cross the log-straddled creek and am alone again with my kerosene lamp under the usual canvas of stars. I have long dreamed on Doug. I am not the only one. Youngest of the Manaroans, he is also the speculative object of what seems like near-universal female fantasy in our small corner of the world, and has had affairs with Sylvie, then Claire. More recently he is rumoured to be in love with Michelle: Punch and Judy puppet operator, married, lives across the Sound.

I try not to think of Doug and feel a lick of excitement at how the mood shifted between us on the ocean. A knock at my caravan door interrupts the jack-knifing of my thought. Murder has infected us. Night elongates its shadow. *I didn't want you to spend tonight alone*, he says. And of that I am glad.

Winter

It is the time of year when the Pines downsizes. Slim people-pickings, diminished visitor intake and slender rations as the core group dwindles to a handful. We move through the dream of days on energy-saver mode, my father and sister not among us. My father has been marooned at the other end of the North Island, delivering my sister for a stay in Dargaville, where my mother has been living the last year or so. He has

come down with hepatitis and is stuck there for the winter, imbibing liver-tonic—dandelion greens and pints of carrot juice—in the house of my mother Christina, Heinz and their two young sons, Krishna and Julius.

Others at Manaroa, where my father evidently contracted the illness, have hepatitis too. Hepatitis A is sweeping the broader hippy community. The Department of Health sends us brochures on diagnosis, incubation period and treatment. Post-mail-boat-run, Kate and Rob, Sylvie, Claire, B. Ware and her lover Gordie and I huddle in the kitchen reading the list of symptoms. Nausea, jaundice, headaches and fatigue. We're all nursing the last two, and Rob has jaundiced eyes. The most fastidious of us all, Phil, is already lying up-paddock beneath his shingled caravan roof with textbook yellow skin. We pore and sweat over the listed symptoms, spontaneously contracting one or another on the spot.

From his sofa post, the most hedonistic of all remains aloof and sanguine. *Die of a misprint*, Bruce cackles, addressing our collective hypochondria between inhalations of bong. Decades of alcohol and marijuana abuse notwithstanding, Bruce hasn't exhibited a single symptom and nor will he.

Man with a dog

It is lonely with so few Manaroans in residence. Without the presence of my father I am unmoored again. Casting about for friend or confidante in the seasonally shrunk, jaundice-stalked Pines, I set my eye on Hooki. Innocent of other people, the Londoner appears not to notice the craft I put into this. He won't disclose his star sign but takes pleasure in exacerbating the community's itch to know. He thinks astrology is rubbish, a short cut to categorisation he'll ensure none take on his behalf. He's not having any truck with the term *hippy* either. Balding at thirty-one, Hooki is an outsider passing through the hirsute fairy tale that is Manaroa.

Even so, my discreet offensive is working. After forging me the dungeon door handle, Hooki begins to drop confidences my way. His bemusement at the community factions and kitchen politics, for one. At other people, full stop. While I have an endless fascination with behaviour, psychology and motive, Hooki would rather not dirty his hands with analysis. He's happy for me to, though—on his account. He will point out some irrational or risible behaviour, rubbery features making great play of his comic stock-in-trade, gob-smacked, and then slyly wait for my opinion.

The pocket mirror Hooki flexes our way renders a comically blunt reflection of community. I am not entirely fooled. Perceiving vulnerability, I offer up best theory. Several even. In this way our mutual entertainment and solicitude are assured. More, I feel *useful*. Almost as useful as Hooki: carpenter, blacksmith and man with a dog.

Rooster

Hooki and I begin to undertake chores together. The day-long operation of heating the copper for the monthly laundry is one such. Hooki beheading the rooster on my behalf, another. The rooster has a thing for women. On the way to the shitter we routinely stall at the back-garden gate, while Rooster patrols the strip between fence line and the brush tepee that houses the can. Best practice is to arm yourself with a length of firewood and take aim as you pass. If you make it without the rooster flying at you, spurs raised, he will hurl himself at the closed door once you are within—just to remind you there is return passage to contemplate. It is intimidating sitting on the can while an avian heavyweight throws himself at the door. Even reliable warriors Kate and B. Ware quail.

Mostly I get by. But, one morning I make the fatal mistake of meeting Rooster's red eye from my side of the garden gate. I am transfixed; passage denied. Happening upon this scene, Hooki decides enough is enough. The rooster's execution by chopping block is swift in comparison to the bullying he has dished out his lifelong. The bloodstained wood chips nudge my vegetarian conscience but only a bit.

After this violent gallantry I draw closer to Hooki and he to me. One night, I sleep in his woodshed mezzanine, cord of firewood stacked below, Jimbo the dog draped across the threshold. For the amount of time you can spend, in a life, fantasising about or engaging in sex, the details are inversely unrecoverable. What I do remember is that something goes wrong in the wood-scented dark. I don't expect Hooki to be so touchy and, then, so quick to bitterness. He doesn't expect me to be such an inexperienced girl. I should write the whole thing off as sexual incompatibility and move on, but this is Manaroa. There is nowhere to move on to.

Slingshot sister

Something else happens that night in the woodshed. Hooki tells me a short, foundational story.

He has a sister, a hellcat older person who had it in for him as a boy. It's England, somewhere in the cold north, but she goes about in shorts with unblemished tomboy legs. *Thin as a streak of piss*, says Hooki. Read: scornful and dynamic. One night, Hooki is reading in bed when his sister comes in and shoots the light out with her slingshot. After plunging book and boy into instant darkness, she leaves. Nary a word exchanged.

Hooki's aggrievement thickens with the decades. Maybe that's why he executes the rooster so summarily. He has long kept a victim's outrage warm. By the time he arrives at Manaroa, random malice is central to Hooki's theory of others—women in particular. Maybe that is why he chooses me, a girl, as his girlfriend. The original antagonist, no less, albeit in more deceptively pliant costume.

Hooki's story is short, brutal and built on non sequitur. This is the moment Hooki secures my loyalty. With the vanity of the young, I am sure I can salve the wound. And besides, black humour is one of the keys to my heart. I don't realise it, but I am hooked on Hooki's narrative.

Cockteaser

Hooki plunges his van down a steep off-road access to the sea. A few bays along from Manaroa we pitch a tent, fish for snapper and barbecue our catch for dinner and then breakfast. Navigating the tracts of silence that are Hooki's natural habitat is tricky but makes our economical conversation all the more prized. On the way back up the sandy incline from our campsite, the wheels of the van bog. We build tracks of driftwood and sticks and sing Beatles songs until the tyres grip. I am good in a crisis, decides Hooki. He sounds surprised.

Encouraged by misadventure, we take the long road out of the Sounds a few weeks later. The first night we settle in a Motueka campsite where, as luck would have it, a pea-picking machine begins work at midnight in the adjacent field and only completes its industrial din at dawn. We don't seem to be talking as we did at Manaroa on our companionable to-and-fros from the Land, buckets swinging from our hands. On the road, a new horizon of consumer choices unfolds and my natural pickiness about where and when to eat, my opinions about the aesthetics of anything and everything, madden and bewilder Hooki. In an alien landscape our misalignment signals back to us everywhere we look.

In Nelson we share a medical appointment and I give Hooki's star sign the sneaky eye as he reluctantly writes out his birth date for the receptionist. Who else would be this fiercely contrarian, this allergic to the provision of personal data? Only the publicity-shy Virgo. The medical consultation is for contraception. Even we can see that the withdrawal method is unsustainable. In the doctor's room, where I answer nearly all the questions on my own, I am stalked by another, undisclosed question. What am I thinking, attempting to make a couple with this non-disclosing man-alone?

Back at the Pines we argue, then climb the fence of the Omelette Eater's empty villa to have make-up sex in a shaded English garden. It is harder than you might think to find a bed amidst the polished leaves, damp grass and leaf pile. I am wearing my new diaphragm but with difficulty. The V word strikes again as it is wont to do whenever I'm unable to persuade myself of erotic interest. *Vaginismus.* I can barely say it out loud.

In the ballroom that night, alone with Hooki in front of the fire, I swerve away from sex at the last moment. I have ceased to be attracted to him but I don't know how to navigate the feeling. Then, at last minute, I do. The feeling exerts its will. My will. *Cockteaser*, scowls Hooki. The concept fuels his fury. He's had enough of not enough. *Cockteaser* sounds sluttish and quite interesting actually.

Feelings

It's hot and tedious cutting bracken. My double-weight community-chest rayon doesn't breathe and keeps getting snagged. I'm pestering Hooki about something. Feelings probably. I only talk of feelings when real ones have fled the scene. Are unspeakable or not allowed. Maybe I've just been sarcastic. Hooki has a low threshold for female scorn. Maybe I remind him of his sister.

Hooki and I don't exchange confidences anymore because we are no longer innocent bystanders or understanding third parties in each other's lives. Coupled, we have become culpable in everything that the other registers as wrong. It's easy to hit a nerve. I do this all the time now, hit exposed nerves. It's like toothache: your tongue keeps checking to see if the loose tooth waggles, if it hurts as much as it did the first time. It does.

With practised swing Hooki turns and sics his sickle through the air above the bracken, the family talent for taking aim manifest. I duck and feel the *whoosh* as it parts the air next to my ear. The realisation connects a few cold seconds after the sickle fails to: I have to leave Hooki. Manaroa. The whole malnourished hippy trip. There's nothing here for a girl like me, nothing for any kind of girl as far as I can see, for as far as the eye can see. In fact, I am the only girl here and that, in itself, is wrong.

My father and sister have still not returned from the north, from my father's prolonged date with illness and, as it happens, my mother. I know my sister will be happy for this unforeseen embroidery on the family chapter, and I sense my father will be more at home than he cares to admit. Consuming his liver-cure dandelion greens. Spidering the pages of consecutive exercise-book journals. Sleeping on a ticking mattress encircled by loosed organic oranges—part of the decorative scheme *and* available to eat. My mother has come a long way in her arrangements and settings since the bleak stages of the haunted Waiheke Island house. There are cooling harmonies to be found in the way she constructs an interior, even that of another dumpy ex-farmhouse set down in a run of thistled Dargaville paddock. She will be in the narrow north-facing bathroom where the light is good, leather apron over her velvets, covering a canvas in impasto layers.

It is late Wednesday when Hooki has his violent fit of pique. I pack a bag. Pretty much the only objects I have acquired or hung on to since first arriving at my father's Floodhouse are two ornithological guides from Morth, the kindly, moth-like husband of Maureen; a Royal Winton flowered jug; and my two sable brushes. I don't take any of these. And although I think I will recover them—along with the *Encyclopaedia of Birds*, bursting with colour plates, that I purchased on layby from Kirkcaldie & Stains with pocket money from Granny Margaret—I never do.

On Friday, I travel light on the mail boat out. I'm heading north to Wellington to be an illustrator. At least, that is the plan. My father has left me to my fate and, finally, I have the temerity to seize it by the scruff of its neck.

PART 4
Modern world

City Limits

I am sleeping in the mezzanine bed of a high-gloss red converted garden shed in the back yard of the Lotus Yoga Centre, Aro Street, Wellington. High gloss goes better in red; I am inordinately proud of this new sleepout. I don't do yoga and nor do my flatmates Steve, Linda, David or acid-casualty Chris, all of whom live in the property's scatter of secular share-houses.

Once a week, Linda and Steve, who are an item, and their journalist friend Tom Scully eat at the Gold Coin on upper Willis Street—an exercise in cultivated irony, MSG and everything fried. I am number four at the fluoro-lit table, learning to love the free plate of buttered white bread cut on the diagonal, nemesis of my wholegrain parents, that comes with every order of sweet and sour.

By day I go to work. I have bluffed my way into a position as baker at Natural Juices, an inner-city café when these are still exotic in the capital, soon to become City Limits. Fruit nectar isn't the right signifier for New Wave let alone punk rock, which is where the scene is heading. Move over, Joni; here come the Slits, the Modern Lovers and the Durutti Column. Owner and till-man Warwick gives me my first proper job after I walk in off the street and ask after work. With a genial counter style and the twitchy dexterity of a man with a fast metabolism, Warwick blinks and appraises me. *What can you bake?*

A quick scan of the memory archives reveals a few scaled-up desserts to feed Manaroa numbers. The ubiquitous apple and berry crumble, a yoghurt quince pie. *Everything*, I reply with the bravado of extreme youth, trusting in my loaves and fishes experience in the Pines kitchen.

As it happens there is a vacancy. As it happens my latter-day Depression cook experience serves me well. Warwick and I share the early morning shift. He is John Hadwen's cousin but that doesn't help my cause. *Are you Christian?* he asks one day. My grandmother once used the same formulation to pass admiring comment on my talent for peace-brokering. In Warwick's case I understand the insult it is intended to be. Hippies don't fare any better in his estimation. I have landed amidst a different kind of disaffected. It helps that they are urban and scintillatingly fashion-conscious.

Damn your eyes, is the dishwasher–dancer's stock riposte to lunching civil servants and hipster musicians alike. Straight-spined in Doc Martens, Andrea stalks the floor with the dirties. As thrilling as she is terrifying, we are hostage to her evil chic and ruddy cheekbone apples.

Then there is Dale, who cooks everything I don't. With his tomb-straight jet hair, paper-white skin and sarcastic sashay for the astral cameras, Dale is the first queen I have encountered. I take admiring notes across the stainless steel worktop. And yet. Dale may be famous for the hand-spun aioli in his salade niçoise, and his French onion soup, but my yoghurt quince pie sells out as soon as it is plated.

Life studies

Thanks to Andrea, and a torn plastic shopping bag thrust my way at the end of the lunchtime traffic, I am looking more credible. *Here, I'm too big-boned for this shit*, the dishwasher says, attempting to muffle her generosity. Inside is a gold-and-black-striped Lurex jumper, a pale green organdie day dress, and a dirty-pink, forties crêpe number with a drop-waist. My flatmate Linda chops the green organdie into my first mini dress. Then she runs up an all-purpose black mini skirt, which I team with the Lurex. I'm feeling Very New Wave.

Photographer friend Janet Bayly takes a series of Polaroids of me in the Botanical Gardens Begonia House. It is she who claims that only egoists wear all white. Here I am, camera-shy in pink crêpe, a graphic design student now.

And there I am in the Lurex, in the front yard of my new Bidwill Street share house, across the road from the polytech, in a photograph taken by Linda. She, Steve and I have moved here after our Aro Street days—and mutual tolerance between ourselves and the Lotus Yoga Centre landlord—came to an abrupt end.

There's another series of photographs from this time, in which I am wary in a diamante necklace and nothing else. For a single session I am a photographer's nude model. These photographs are paradoxical, baring all and disclosing nothing. On a gap between his commercial assignments, the photographer wishes to pay homage to Edward Weston's nudes. He observes perfect form, but I regret the risk I take descending into his hermetically sealed basement. Long after I've spent the six crisp twenties that he hands me on completion of the two-hour session, a reinforced brown envelope of duotones appears in my letterbox. I stow the photographs in a cigar box. Fifteen years on, I will send one in a love letter to Jeremy Clegg—a boy who knew me then, and the man with whom I live now.

Modelling for life-drawing classes at Wellington Polytechnic, I wear Grandmother Susan's diamantes again. Maybe she

would have been appalled. Maybe she would have enjoyed this derangement of middle-class decorum: she was a painter, after all. I wear the diamantes around the clock, to bed. My commune training in naked horticulture is standing me in good stead. For twenty dollars an hour all I have to do is roll out of bed; apply kohl eyeliner, Andrea's pink, crêpe, footless tights and embroidered Chinese slippers; and cross the road to shed it all again.

The work of the poses—finding them, holding them, surviving them—is engaging. It helps that I am unselfconscious about my body. On the movable stage, I take on cat-like self-sufficiency. I like the respectfully sustained focus of the room, the tamped-down awareness of private struggle unfolding on A2 sheets of paper as each participant's focus deepens the collective concentration. Later, I will find something similar at work on a film set.

I feel able to pose for the classes of Kate Coolahan, a famous printmaker of pensive authority and a debonair haircut, because I am not yet enrolled in the graphic design diploma. After a number of sessions, she remarks that my body reminds her of someone. Dispensing with languor, I rush downstairs to the library to look up Manet's *Olympia*. A cursory glance and I discount the resemblance. Olympia is a creamy-skinned courtesan on propped pillows, ankles crossed above satin mules, one of which has slipped off on the flowery shawl on which she lies. She turns her naked body slightly outward, one hand resting on her thigh, the better to observe the viewer. Manet's is a realist portrait of a young woman with a softly upholstered body. *Too chubby*, is what I think.

These days, I am quite prepared to accept the gift of resemblance in body proportions and pose. An artist acquaintance with

whom I sometimes do rounds of the local park with our dogs—a pug, a porgie and a whippet—scoffs. *She's not very striking. It would have been her look back that your teacher was thinking of. That's what that painting is famous for.*

It is true that I enjoyed watching the students as they worked. Once, I unintentionally caught a tall, safety-pin-festooned boy off guard in Kate's class by appearing naked at his side, on the break, to look at his drawing. He was munching an apple; I thought we were used to each other by now. *For God's sake, Miro, put some clothes on*, he hissed. I had forgotten the new rules of decorum I was living under; that, absurdly enough, they applied even in the life-drawing room, even with would-be punk rockers. It would be years before I realised that the sartorially radical are often—socially, in their values—quite tame.

Manet's painting ghosts me in other ways. I live with Nestor, the whippet, who, in habitual elegance, disposes himself just like Olympia. Recumbent on his side, thin red collar at throat, high-heeled paws crossed, he leans slightly back to regard me, his human.

Olympia nudges another likeness for Kate Coolahan, another model. This is Christina, my mother, who posed in the same rooms for Kate's life-drawing class. She was a design school student twenty years before I become one, before I was born, maybe even before I was conceived. I do nothing with Kate's revelation except take it away and treasure it.

The design school faculty ask me back to model for a second year. By now I have crossed the floor, uncannily like my mother before me, and am a student myself. I agree on the condition that I model for any class but my own. When I turn up for the second years in a pair of leopard-spot boot-style slippers, Kate asks me to leave them and the diamante necklace on. Later that term, when I pass a wall of nudes in the company of my classmates, I enjoy the secret of the accessorised model's identity. Some of the drawings are really good. I share this thrill with my two new post-punk friends, Phil Kelly and Jeremy Clegg.

My own experience of drawing tuition is less enlightening than the classes of Kate Coolahan or of the only other woman in the department, Susan Skerman. With his coal-black eyes and harrowed elegance, Ron Burt must once have been a streak of something interesting. Now, he holds us in unhappy thrall to his withering silences and our collective inability to please. Thanks to his pedantic insistence on shading, the eschewal of outline, and the calculation of relative lengths via thumb measurements marked out on a pencil held latitudinally to the eye, my intuitively rhythmic feeling for line is undone.

Cinnamon and nutmeg

Living in the city of my childhood, independent of my grandmother and with a flat and social capital of my own, I am confident enough to restore relations. Every few weekends I put on an op-shop mini skirt of napless midnight blue in which I feel especially mysterious and walk across town to 46A to sit in the grey club armchair across from Martin and eat Margaret's tinned-spaghetti pizza from a plate in my lap. Cordial satisfactions, these.

Sometimes, a little violent hole opens, a grief for the intimate past with my grandmother, who now behaves like a Distant Lady. I take this hole back to the autonomy of my

Bidwill Street room where it hollows and recedes. This is a room of beautiful bay windows into which waft draughts of cinnamon and nutmeg from the Empire Spice factory on Hopper Street below.

The last time I see Hooki

The last time I see Hooki is in the room of the bay windows, where he crashes on his way north. Hooki doesn't know it yet but he's on the way to becoming a Christian. But first, disembarking off the Cook Strait ferry and making straight for my unfamiliar address, he assumes the hospitality of my bed. He doesn't seem to realise that there is more than an ocean between us now. I haven't the heart to tell him.

As soon as Hooki has fallen asleep, I climb out of bed, out the bedroom window, onto the unstable top floor balcony that looks out over a dishevelled three-tier garden, and into my flatmate's window. There, I fool around with Lotus Yoga Centre Steve. This serial flatmate is a better kisser than his Bukowski pretensions would suggest. He kisses like a girl, long and swoony. I kiss him back in kind. The loveliness sets me straight. Kissing is one of life's sweet things; I'm only just discovering that.

Before dawn, I crawl out Steve's window, through mine and back into my bed where Hooki slumbers—or appears to. He always did have a good poker face. He affects a daybreak waking. Just in time for the Palmerston North bus but not for toast or conversation. And just like that, I slough Hooki off like an old skin.

Negative space

I don't know it yet but I'm about to fall in love with a design school student in a waistcoat of zippered mushroom-coloured fur. The waistcoat is the detachable lining of a gentleman's coat. The boy is Philip Kelly: bass guitarist, singer and my first boyfriend. At last, a boy my own age. It is Phil who spots the zip-up leopard-spot slippers on a lunchtime forage at the Newtown Salvation Army, where we have gone with our constant third, Jeremy. Zips loom large in our lexicon.

Wellington Polytechnic doesn't give me a profession as planned, or even many skills—at least not those intended. I am studious. I am commended for possessing an eye for negative space and composition. At year's end, however, a bunch of Cs (and a few concessional Bs) are crowned by a D for professional attitude. Presumably for failing to accord the proper respect to the conceptual notion of the client—we never actually meet one, so this *is* notional. Implicitly, to the ageing male staff, too. *You must think you're at art school.* A teacher actually says this when I attempt to initiate discussion in class. In the unyielding hierarchy that is Visual Communication Design it is dangerous to express unsolicited opinion or give voice. The older and more politic, of whom there are only a few, confine their protest to visual language. To the page or to their style or dress. If the expressive force of these sublimations fails to satisfy, they leave. A short-lived ally of mine takes up a basketball scholarship in America. But for man and boy alike the boundaries are more expansive, the judgements less punitive.

Privately, I think the D is for getting pregnant and having an abortion. This happens twice, contraception notwithstanding. I am fatally fertile. I have blotted my copybook with sexuality.

Female sexuality. On reflection, it might have been more problematic to get an A for professional attitude.

Pregnancy

After the first positive pregnancy test, my father appears to camp on my bedroom floor and accompany me on the long walks up towards the Newtown town belt, in whose shadow the abortion clinic nestles. My condition has outgrown the ministrations of the nurses at the polytech health clinic. There are further examinations and appointments, all respectfully conducted by female health professionals, to navigate before the procedure. Strung between morning sickness and strange cravings, I let my father shout me sausage rolls and cream doughnuts on our otherwise comfortless walks home.

I talk to the foetus in the privacy of my own head. *You can't stay*, I say, as gently but firmly as I can. *I have no place for you.* I have been compelled to admit that I am barely coping myself. It is as if I am talking to the wind or a small breeze. After a while the feeling comes over me; the foetus hears my intention. Some kind of love passes between us. Some kind of unfinished sympathy. However painfully, I have stated my truth.

On the afternoon after the foetus is unstuck from my womb, I lie on my side in the recovery room, cramping. It will be like a heavy period, the nurses tell me.

Later, my father takes a photo of me standing on the white embroidered bedroom rug at Bidwill Street. We wish to mark the occasion. I am in a nightie with detaching hem lace at the knee, a cardigan over. My mother stitched this nightie from a cotton flour sack, dyed it pink, and embroidered a vertical line of flowers between the breasts. It is a rare gift of hers,

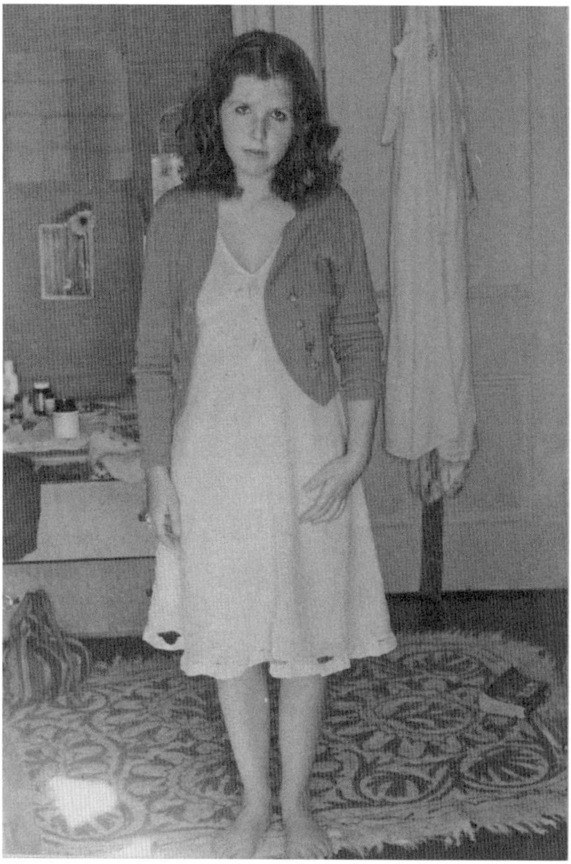

one that I wear and wear. I stand squarely in the middle of the picture, looking directly out at my father–photographer. I have bare feet and my head is tilted questioningly towards my left shoulder, one hand inclining loosely towards the centre of my body. The colours of spring are in my costume and in the room. It is an unmistakeably sad photograph but resolute; in my expression I see the burden of awareness.

After a few days my father goes home, and I go back to polytech.

In the post-procedure wastelands into which I drift, the ex-advertising men, the alcoholic drawing teacher from whom I am unlearning how to draw, the fields of gouache that will never lay flat as they are supposed to, cease to signify much.

The shine goes out of nude modelling, the confident return of my gaze to those who draw my body recedes and turns inward. I will have to give it up. A textile design student in a Rosie the Riveter headscarf enquires directly about my health. We are sunning our legs on the tech concrete at morning tea after they have invited me, their model, to join them. She's had a dream that I'm in trouble. Only weeks out from the abortion, I am in trouble, but there's not much I can do about it. I don't confide in Rosie the Riveter, but her dreamer's concern ameliorates some of the raw exposure I feel and allies my body's mute grieving.

I do confide in Sue Skerman because I am her favourite model, so she says, and because I am about to let this modest, outspoken woman down. I feel unusual anxiety about letting people down. It is as if I have engineered a symbolic separation from which neither party will recover. *Will they forgive me? Will I see them again?* I do not confide this anxiety to Sue, only the termination. Sue's warmth flows towards me, briefly alleviating the bleak climate within.

*

Into this lonely space walks Phil. He comes from a family of women—three sisters, one of whom is a nurse, and a solo mother—and has the emotional gravity to go with it. His mother, enjoying the lexicon of the young female factory workers she serves tea to, calls him a *spunk*. I am suspicious of the word but I know they are right. I tell Phil about the abortion. Alone in the field of conservative children that is first year Visual Communications Design, Phil is engaged, unshockable, a salve. We talk and talk.

Love

Polytech was right to fail me even if it did so for the wrong reason. I will never make a Neville Brody, whose layouts and typography my new friends pore over in *Face* magazine. A very bored graphic designer is what I would be. What the institution does give me, however, is two great, real-world loves.

After Phil turns up at my kitchen door and I tell him about my termination, we become girlfriend and boyfriend. There is a party at my flat where, alone in the small-hours living room, Phil and I draw ever closer. Into our slow-creep intimacy blows a hippy blow-in called Bodhi. Stopping in front of us, he intones, *Boys just wanna get their rocks off.* When Bodhi decides to stay put, our uninvited witness, we move out onto the unsteady balcony and have a giggle instead. Bodhi has given us his unwitting blessing.

Near dawn, we climb back in the window. My father is sleeping on a mattress on the floor. It doesn't matter as much as you'd think. Phil and I have many reasons to take it slow, to lie blissfully in each other's arms. To chastely swoon.

My poor father.

Only months after the first, my second pregnancy and termination is to Phil. It is even harder than the first. Unable to bring myself to enter into relationship with the foetus, I harden. Once again, I do not feel I have the emotional or material means to raise a child. Maybe it is a question of spirit: I am so much more afraid of what I now know, and of what I do not know too.

Is there a relationship between these depressive sublimations and the complications the procedure is subject to: the infection and further surgery?

In Wellington public hospital, where I am readmitted a day or so after the abortion, I am placed in a ward of women going into or coming out of hysterectomies: a point of miserable incongruity and increasing chill between all. My bedfellows complain to Matron when Phil nestles into me on the pillows as we wait to see if my temperature will settle. If fertility and reproduction are a sore point for these older women, abortion and sexuality are touchpaper sensitive. It is hard to resist the feeling that my presence is an offence. Small but symbolic moments amplify in an environment in which each of us women have made tough decisions, and in which a current of collective but deeply private mourning is strong.

Through it all there is Phil. Phil is my first love. In adoration and its return, I find anchor and rare certainty. Sweetness too. Phil and I will live in and out of each other's pockets, across the fence, the road, the campus and, finally, the hall for the next seven years. Insomniacs both, we keep separate beds to retreat to, to toss alone in. *I love you / I spurn you / We live in a clamp* is a very short lyric I write sometime in our fifth year together.

Young animals

The other love blooms late, when I am living in another city in another country, but the germ of it lies in that single seminal year at polytech when I am at the eye of the stormy forces of life and death. And rebirth too.

Jeremy is the boy who sews himself into his black stovepipes to get a better fit one morning before 3-D design class. The boy who dyes his hair leopard spot using a tri-selection of chemist-shop colour and holes scissored in a shower cap. When Jeremy runs, he *does* look like a leopard, I think, although he assures me that he is actually quite slow. Sometimes he comes to class blue-fingered, straight from surfing the icy waters of Lyall Bay. I watch the way he disappears when he smokes a joint and disapprove as only an astral-travelling ex-hippy could.

Phil thinks that, of all of the design school students, Jeremy makes it look easy. He is an inspired visual thinker, it is true, but I have had a whiff of the excoriating self-criticism that belies relations between his hand and eye.

I souvenir an etching of his.

In it, outsize pink dentures grin above power-suited shoulders as wide as the landscape format that contains them. The savage control, the way the ravening dentures stand for the missing head, is bold. Soon, this boy of modesty, daring and apocalyptic imagination is off to London, where he will work in a sandwich shop, avoid the New Zealand crowd and, eventually, study post-graduate illustration at Central Saint Martin's College.

Our courtship does not take place for another decade, but I took note long before. It begins at a party held by Phil, with whom

I have long since amicably split. It takes root in letters between London and Sydney, where Jeremy and I respectively live. The envelopes and parcels from England are so richly stencilled, overdrawn and inked that sometimes the petite Madagascan postal clerk at my local post office does not want to hand them over. It puts down roots in serial apartments across Sydney, a ruinously expensive city in which the resourceful low-income renter must find cracks in the real estate strata. In the case of Jeremy and me, in overlooked eyries above shops and once, above a luxury car showroom.

It would be unfair not to mention Nestor, the canine Olympia with red choker and brindled coat. In the deco apartment—with its many dog's-eye beds—in which Jeremy and I eventually settle, Nestor commands our wonder and esteem by doing everything he does with his *whole* body. Just past adolescence, this young whippet is serpentine in eating, greeting, motion and feeling. After two years as Nestor's dedicated observer it occurs to me that I take pleasure in this as I once did, at discreet remove, in another's young animal grace. The grace belonged to Jeremy Clegg in an oversized fisherman's jersey, Wellington Polytechnic, 1982.

PART 5
For the record

Archiving

One day the Floodhouse appears on Salesman John's unofficial itinerary. He must have been directed to our house via word of mouth. Either that or my father gets talking to him, a rare interloper at Canvastown General Store and, sensing a latent dropout with insufficient nerve, invites him home for soya bean omelette with kelp, and dandelion coffee. I don't know how this nerdy stranger gets these hefty delicacies down—his sales car is papered with the wrappers of junk food eaten on the fly—but, as I soon find out, Salesman John is an amiable contrarian, dry but submissive. After the first visit, he adds the Floodhouse to his rounds.

Dressed head to toe in brown nylon and with heavy rectangular glasses, Salesman John speaks mainly though his camera, eloquence only a shutter-click away. Viewfinder glued to eye, the travelling salesman makes culture raids on the South Island hippy community from the convenience of his photocopier-catalogue-stacked company car. Despite his mix of personal concealment and voyeurism, he is tolerated. After all, he is just another transient in a world where personal biography is rarely broached.

I know the jokes about zoom lenses and substitute phallic extensions but, plastic polymer crimes against fashion notwithstanding, I empathise with Salesman John. I have my own awkwardness. Besides, there is nothing I like more than to pore over his frontline feeds of assertive hippy Madonnas and their men, soaking up their cues in black and white.

Sometimes, I allow him to drive me down to the Canvastown store to buy half a pound of butter, or down the highway and along a road bulldozed across paddocks to a local farmer's milking shed, where I exchange a few coins for milk, still warm and frothing from the udder, decanted into my father's battered aluminium pail.

Salesman John's photographs of our corner of the world, grainy black-and-white prints he develops and distributes as calling cards, are unique. No one else I know has a camera; the contemporary photographic record seems non-existent; and so I begin collecting these five-by-sevens. Stained with poorly mixed fixative, their imagery is stern but lovely. Indelible too, despite darkroom haste. With barely a smile adorning the faces of his subjects, his prints have the aura of ancestral portraits. In time to come, these knocked-off souvenirs will assume the importance of a minor anthropological record, their cultural data one of the only visual records of a vanished people and place. My people and place.

1

Salesman John gives me a lift the forty or so miles home from Tahuna. Chaperoned by Sally Everett, I have hitchhiked to visit John of Saratoga, but not found him in residence. Before I leave the commune, the salesman takes a snap of me as I look up and straight down the barrel from inspecting a fan of his prints in the tatty grounds. I am in my weekend uniform of wash-shrunk Wellington Girls' cardy, embroidered peasant blouse and gored skirt, a clay bead on a leather string at my neck. Fixed in Salesman John's bromide, I have an undefended stare, surprise escaping cupid bow lips.

2

A year on from the stolen Tahuna moment, my vestigial puppy fat is gone and my school education complete. I am caught turning in profile by Salesman John's camera, black circle skirt with Japanese mountains swirling at gumbooted ankles. I am the only defined thing in the primeval slosh of track that merges into a muddy bank. This is Saratoga, a journey by water from Manaroa, where I now live. The thin black strap crossing my back ends in a cloth bag that contains—what exactly? A hairbrush, an extra hair band, no doubt, for I am always losing them, but no money, no more complex female effects.

3

Is badly printed. Chemical flowers spatter an underexposed back and arse; float across the picture plane like plankton. I am squatting, turned towards the entrance to a sea cave, hair wavy-wet, naked after a swim in the icy waters of Schoolhouse Beach. My sister stoops as she emerges from rocky shadows. Blond Kim, her back turned, is the other framing nymph. The scene feels submerged, private, without sound, as if taking place on the sea floor.

4

Taken minutes after the previous photograph, this is only a stone's throw along the shore. Here, Claire folds herself into calico-clad crouch on the pebble-cold beach, her eyes gunslinger narrow, her lit cigarette biding time.

5

Hooki wears heavily patched trousers, beanie and sweater and clasps a solder-patched enamel mug. In his other hand he raises a stick for which his retriever Jimbo leaps, as vertical and economical as a black calligraphic brushstroke. Kim stands nearby on the sloping paddock, hands on hips, exulting in the show. Unhitched from horse, a dray downs its driftwood shafts behind her. Mist decapitates the Manaroa hills.

6

Overseen by Sylvie, Hooki applies first aid to the Pines bathroom window. If Hooki has stumbled into our frame, there hovers a feeling it could be the wrong one. This only intensifies my interest; this, and his tin ear for other people and what they think of him—and his pre-emptive sensitivity to both.

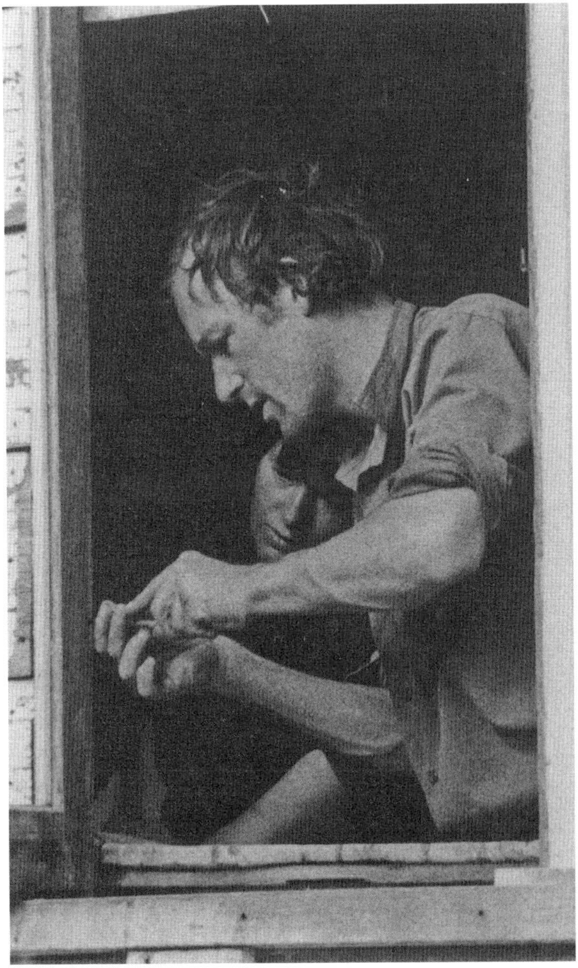

7

Doug of the cloudy hair, side-lit in homage to stubborn male beauty. Even in black and white, his cheek—tactile.

Photograph not taken

We travel by boat from Manaroa to a party at Saratoga, the tiny fishing settlement sometime-resident John has taken for his name. The party house is set along the shorefront among a motley of cottages. Zlatka also lives here. A Slavic beauty who sleeps in a driftwood bed built by her lover Steve, Zlatka flies back and forth to Sydney to model. Such commercial dexterity is unknown in our world. Steve is one of the three brothers renowned for their carpentry and for possessing the kind of looks that might have been rendered by Byzantine icon painters. Stuck on these scant facts, and on her legendary slashes for cheekbones, I elaborate Zlatka into a kind of Marlborough Sounds Lady of the Lake.

There are no photographs to back these mythological fragments. But there might have been. In this photograph not taken, I am stepping naked out of the sea. Salesman John is standing on the shore, finger poised on the shutter release. It is a surprise to see him there—but his opportunism is never less than prompt when it comes to pictures.

Hey! Don't you dare exploit her like that, yells Sally Everett, my unsolicited protector, striding down the beach. Proud of my post–whooping cough weight and new breasts, I wouldn't have minded being exploited, actually. Standing between the male voyeur and Zlatka's house, however, Sally literally occupies the moral high ground. I say nothing. Salesman John meekly lowers his camera. He has a strong eye for composition, and the short depth of field that he favours throws his subjects deeper into the moment. The irony is that his untaken snap vividly preserves, in my memory's eye, how confident I felt that day, crashing out of the waves at Saratoga.

Return

In years to come, Manaroa's power of suggestion is so forceful it is the only actual, real-time geography that resembles itself in my dreams. In dream I repeatedly return. The ravelling trip over water by mail boat, the first sight of remembered hills from the sea, the revelation of who will be waiting on the wind-whipped pier all look, sound and feel like themselves. After that, the visions pare off into surreal parallel realms. Caravan floorboards disport waist-high grass and unfamiliar occupants. And there are Christian others in the smoky kitchen, as if in semblance of a proper commune with proper rules. Return is narcotic: tantalising and deranging hope. Dreams of lost homes and homelessness and yearning are cornerstone dreams for me. This is one more.

I return only once in physical time to Manaroa. I have a life in Wellington now and return to show it off to those who remain. This and my new-found years. On the mail boat I fall in with the peripatetic Salesman John who, as usual, engages through his viewfinder. I keep the two black-and-white eight-by-tens he takes of me, once landed, for my collection.

I am proud of my new, urban look: kohl eyes, sixties sundress, footless tights and embroidered Chinese slippers. One glance at the kohl and Bruce dourly comments that I look like a Moroccan boy. The reference is one of the sly upsetters he trades in. We are standing on the muddy track to the Land, where Bruce is taking smoko from working on the timber frame of that malingering group project, the New House. I had hoped to be prodigal in return. Bruce's comment mires me straight back in the unhappy insignificance of a scene in which I am forever fixed as a child. With hindsight it might have been a compliment—more likely, it flatters Bruce's cosmopolitan status. I don't stay long. As Jonathan Richman sings, *I'm in love with the modern world now.*

Mythologies

I once had a woman friend whom another dubbed *romantically agile* for her apparent ease in gliding seamlessly from one long, live-in relationship to another. Light on her feet, a dancer, I envied Alison her smooth transitions. My own agility has concerned comparatively fast turn-around entrances and exits of a different kind, and the transitions have been far from smooth.

The adult society my father and his rural hippy friends invited me into offered deceptively egalitarian access that was heaven, hell and a limbo of ennui in between. I've experienced nothing since that resembles it. The rural poverty, elemental splendour and physical labour; the oddball charisma of the people and their outmoded props; the idealistic break with authorities and certainties—the valour; and even the difficult politics of the commune, combined into a heady elixir. The dress-ups—those gritty, ethereal textiles—only contributed to the efficacy with which the scene staged itself.

I was a young animal, hyper receptive to the beauty and contradiction of the world. I was not alone. We were drunk on mythologies.

I don't feel moralistic about this. Most of my life I've been slipstreaming some form of mythology. A person or atmosphere caught on the fly becomes the subject of more sustained musing or dreaming, or merely a moment that drops into vertical time. The Manaroans offered a collective intensification of my predisposition for this. I know there are dangers in such an inclination, and some of them become manifest in this recounting. Strengths too.

Now even more than then I appreciate the green consciousness at work in our lack of cars, our stringent consumption, our constant gardening. Our collective footprint was tiny, wittingly so. The slow-time, the harmonies we enjoyed as a result—the green fumes—you breathed them in—obliviated any sense of lack we might otherwise have felt.

There's something else. The inverse relation of sexual joy to experimentation and boundary crossing has troubled me as I write. I have wished it could be otherwise—for my past self and for the reader. To this I would like to add that this lack was a precursor to later richer experience. To be moved by desire rather than desirability was the key. In this simple reversal of the equation, sex got a whole lot better for me. The discovery of agency took a lot of fumbling and misfires, as these pages record. To provide witness to those missteps, my own and others', seemed the honest and necessary thing to do. Meanwhile, cellular joy vested itself elsewhere.

And it really did.

Notes

Harold Wilson

Ardizzone, E. (1965) *Tim and Ginger*. London: Oxford University Press.

On my father's side

Wordsworth, W. (1805). 'The Prelude XII'. Accessed January 26, 2019, from https://www.rc.umd.edu/editions/poets/texts/preludeXII.html.

I have repurposed Wordsworth's 'Spots of Time': 'There are in our existence spots of time / That with distinct pre-eminence retain / A renovating virtue . . .'

Punctum

Barthes, R. (1984). *Camera Lucida*. (p. 27). London: Fontana Paperbacks.

'This second element which will disturb the *studium* I shall therefore call *punctum*; for *punctum* is also: sting, speck, cut, little hole—and also a cast of the dice. A photograph's *punctum* is that accident which pricks me (but also bruises me, is poignant to me).'

The word

Hall, D., & Oates, J. (1976). Rich Girl. On *Bigger Than Both of Us*. USA: RCA Records.

Felder, D., Henly, D., & Frey, G. [The Eagles]. (1977). Hotel California. On *Hotel California.* USA: Asylum Records.

John of Saratoga

Lang, A (ed.) (1967). *The Blue Fairy Book.* New York: Dover. (Original work published 1889).

Hopper, D. (1969). *Easy Rider.* Los Angeles: Raybert Productions / Pando Company.

Affinities

Solnit, R. (2020). Recollections of my non-existence. London: Granta. p 220.

Rebecca Solnit traverses the spectrum of gendered entitlement in her essay-gone-viral, 'Men Explain Things to Me' (2012). As she herself is quick to point out, however, the term 'mainsplaining' is mistakenly attributed to her, and was, in fact, coined by an anonymous commentator in response.

In passing

Dickinson, E. letter to Higginson, T. W. In *A Choice of Emily Dickinson's Verse.* (p. 10). London: Faber and Faber.

'Friday I tasted life. It was a vast morsel. A circus passed the house—still I feel the red in my mind.'

Fifteen

Dylan, B. (1976). *Desire.* New York City: Columbia Records.

'Scorpio sphinx in a calico dress' is a line in 'Sara', the song Bob Dylan wrote for his wife.

Miss Johnson

Elliot, T. S. (1961). The Love Song of J. Alfred Prufrock. *Selected Poems.* (p. 13). London: Faber and Faber.

The last time I saw Richard

Mitchell, J. (1971). The last time I saw Richard. On *Blue.* California: Reprise Records.

On my mother's side

Simpson, P. (2019). *Colin McCahon: There Is Only One Direction: Vol. 1, 1919–1959.* New Zealand: Auckland University Press.

Two photographs in the Hocken Library featuring Patrick Hayman with Colin McCahon, Elespie Forsyth, Doris Lusk and Rodney Kennedy attest to their friendship.

Last days of Wellington Street

Amis, M. (1995) *The Information*. London: Flamingo.

'Julie and Robert brought home the Information,' by which I mean the Martin Amis sense of *prime* information.

Floating again

Shakespeare, W. (2019). *Measure for Measure.* Act 3, Sc 1. Accessed February 7, 2019, on https://www.sparknotes.com/nofear/shakespeare/measure-for-measure/page_120/

'Heaven shield, my mother play'd my father fair! / For such a *warped slip of wilderness* [emphasis added] / Ne'er issu'd from his blood.'

Three houses

Potter, B. (2002). *The Tale of the Pie and the Patty-Pan*. London: Penguin. (Original work published 1905).

Who owns the buildings?

Neumann, K. (1958). *The Fly*. Los Angeles: 20th Century Fox.

At work and play

Gibran, K. (1974). *The Prophet*. London: Heinemann.

de Beauvoir, S. (1972). *The Second Sex*. (H. M. Parshley, Trans.) Harmondsworth: Penguin. (Original work published 1949).

Wilhelm, R., & Baynes, C. F. (1968). *The I Ching or Book of changes* (3rd ed.). New York: Pantheon Books.

The Land

After the first edition is published Salesman John contacts me by email. I've not seen him or heard of him since our last encounter on the mailboat some forty years ago. He has over a hundred photographs 'surrounding the events of those days'. Would I like to see them? It is the kind of shock one could do with more of. Salesman John is, in fact, John Lowe, and in the days of which we speak he was a salesman of Philips components not photocopiers and, before that, a travelling technician for Kerridge Odeon cinemas.

Nested in the cascade of black-and-whites—so many that they have to be emailed in eight batches—is a photograph of the newly completed community house. There it stands on The Land with a discarded skirt of planks at its ankles not unlike those bark peelings you find at the base of Paperbark trees in my suburban Sydney neighbourhood: a vision of rebirth. I was wrong to be so doomy; wrong about the timber

frame's ultimate demise; wrong about the misfiring collective effort. Kate and Rob's recycled church windows announcing its northern face, the main-house has risen from the ashes and with it, my view of the efficacy of Manaroan ambition. The house is still standing today, Kate tells me, and is known by the young locals as the Womble House.

Seventeen
Melville, H (1853). *Bartleby* (1968) (p. 17). London: Penguin.

Doug is watering saplings along the border of his land when I call, seeking permission to reproduce his photograph. It is February 2020 and it hasn't rained in Tauranga since Christmas. We share the dry, but the story here in New South Wales is so much worse. The summer of the worst fires in recorded world history: over a billion animals and Australian forest two-thirds the size of New Zealand—extinguished.

Having not seen Doug nor heard word of him since I left Manaroa just shy of four decades ago, I'm keeping my expectations low. Mobile pressed to my ear I discover he is a new grandfather, single, a climate change activist and member of Extinction Rebellion. If such a movement had existed—and *we'd got our shit together*—so might the Manaroans have been.

Was Doug always such a good listener? Was I? The work of listening in to the gaps in our conversation—spaces that span unquantifiable amounts of biography, experience and being—is satisfyingly mutual. The past circles and draws us closer—but it is Doug's musing *no beers* that tips us into reflection about sexuality—our sexuality—on the commune.

Honeydew

Coleridge, S. (1816). Kubla Khan. In Bloom, H., & Trilling, L. (eds.), *The Oxford Anthology of English Literature* (1973) (p. 257). New York: Oxford University Press.

Sudden views

Le Guin, U. (1968). *A Wizard of Earthsea*. Middlesex: Puffin Books.

Portals

Michelsen, N. F. (1993). *The American Ephemeris for the 20th Century, 1900–2000 at Midnight.* USA: ACS Publications Inc.

Return

Jonathan Richman and the Modern Lovers (1976). Modern World. On *The Modern Lovers*. California: Beserkely Records.

Life studies

Manet, É. (1863). *Olympia* [oil on canvas]. Musée d'Orsay, Paris.

On occasion I have changed a name to protect the identity of those I write about.

List of illustrations

Acknowledgements

My thanks to

The writer friends who acted as readers or advisors: Martin Edmond, who read over several drafts, gave impeccable notes, and passed on the previously unknown photograph of a young Patrick Hayman in Mapua as reproduced in Peter Simpson's *Colin McCahon: There Is Only One Direction*. Gretchen Shirm, who read a late draft and sent me back to be fairer to the narrator. Janine Creser, friend since the time of the Manaroans, for select readings and confidences. Gail Jones, an early believer and an eloquent speaker on the manuscript's behalf. Michelle de Kretser, Fran Moore, Sophie Cunningham and Mireille Juchau for much-valued advice and solidarity.

My friends Bonnie Elliot and Hans Freymadl for their belief in this project. Peter Sainsbury, an early, enthusiastic respondent to some of these memories, and with whom I made *Floodhouse* (2003), the feature film that prefigured this book. Julie Fortier who encouraged me, years ago in Paris, to write about vaginismus—it only took till now. Robert Fendall for osteopathy beyond the call; Sam Maclean and Woody Naismith of Academy of Film, Theatre and Television for production support; and Joanne Simpson for shepherding the last draft through a round of Australia Council funding.

Fergus Barrowman, who provided a welcome home for my early prose poems in the debut issue of *Sport* and thereafter, and now—wonderfully—this book. Jasmine Sargent for providing the best editing experience—incisive, prudent, generous—I could have wished for. Phil Kelly for designing the cover, and for making himself an unstinting ally of this book. Hao Nguyen for appearing right when I needed him, and for the author photo. Desmond Bovey and Janet Bayly for generous permission to use their photographs in this book.

The Manaroans for the experience and memories; Claire Cannon and Doug Doig, in particular, for their enthusiasm and trust regarding this project, and Kate Jaunay for her salient letters, vivid recall and fact-checking between the first and second editions. John Lowe, aka Salesman John, for his on-the-road photographs of the community.

My mother, Christina Conrad, and father, Norman Bilbrough, for their grace in supporting the notion of this book from the outset, and for occasional additional details. Margaret Beere and Uncle Martin, genies of love and memory. Nestor the whippet, who kept watch while I wrote. And above all, Jeremy Clegg, who did so too.

This project has been assisted by the Australian Government through the Australia Council for the Arts, its arts funding and advisory body.